Salleh Ben Joned

AS I PLEASE
Selected Writings 1975-1994

Introduction
by
Margaret Drabble

Afterword
by
Adibah Amin

SKOOB BOOKS PUBLISHING
LONDON

Introduction   © Margaret Drabble
Afterword   © Adibah Amin
Cover Design   © I.K.Ong
First Published in 1994 by
SKOOB BOOKS PUBLISHING LTD
Skoob PACIFICA Series
11a-17 Sicilian Avenue
off Southampton Row and
Bloomsbury Square
London WC1A 2QH
Fax: 71- 404 4398

ISBN 1 871438 29 2

Agents:
Skoob Books (Malaysia) Sdn Bhd
11 Jalan Telawi Tiga, Bangsar Baru
59100 Kuala Lumpur
Tel/Fax: 603-255 2686

Atrium Publishing Group
11270 Clayton Creek Road
Lower Lake
CA. 95457
Tel: 1-707-995 3906
Fax: 1-707-995 1814

Graham Brash (Pte) Ltd
32 Gul Drive
Singapore 2262
Tel: 65-861 1335, 65-862 0437 Fax: 65-861 4815

Typeset by Pearly Kok. Tel/Fax: 603-255 2686
Printed in Malaysia by POLYGRAPHIC. Fax: 603-905 1553
Colour Separation by Universal Litho Fax: 603-717 7527

I was furious when V.S. Naipaul casually said that mine is " a country without a mind ". But I knew what he meant, and if we confine that remark to the contemporary scene, I couldn't help but agree with him!

Many people have expressed surprise that I was allowed to get away with the kind of things I said in *As I Please* in a country like Malaysia and in an establishment newspaper like the **New Straits Times**. The fact that an intelligent man and a Malay was chief editor, explains the freedom I was tacitly granted. I personally didn't think it was a matter of courage.

Commonsense - that's basically what's needed.

Born on the stroke of midnight, July 4th 1941, and educated in Australia (where his teacher was the distinguished Australian poet James McAuley), Salleh Ben Joned has been a freelance writer since he left the cosy world of Malaysian academia (English Dept., Univ.of Malaya), ten years ago. His first book, a bilingual collection of poems, *Sajak-sajak Saleh: Poems Sacred and Profane*, was published in 1987. *As I Please* is his second book. A substantial volume of poetry, *Adam's Dream*, consisting of old and new poems (English versions of his Malay poems and new poems) is scheduled to appear in 1995.

Salleh has also written a few plays and film scripts, the most important of these being a play in two languages, *Amuk Mat Solo/ The Amok of Mat Solo*. For various reasons, among which is the sensitive nature of its subject and treatment, it has never been staged. *Mat Solo* has been completely rewritten in English. For some years, he has been working on an epic novel in English about an apostate, *Mat Zak*.

He is currently in the U.S.A. as a freelance journalist in rural Pennsylvania. His other preoccupations include minding two screaming kids and killing himself trying to be finally done with the burdensome apostate. *Insha' Allah* - God Willing, the challenging ambience of satanic sexually-harrassed America will prove conducive to the much delayed, much anticipatd birth of one *Mat Zak* as well as his twin brother, the twice-circumcused *Mat Solo*.

SKOOB *Pacifica*

Joint Series Editors: C.Y. Loh & I.K. Ong

To My Malaya *

*In Tagalog, a language related to Malay, the word *malaya* means freedom.

Contents

As I Please

SKOOB *Pacifica* SERIES

in terms of production — the [...] gorgeous lined cover, the types, its so-called editing (in the 2nd section esp.), — this poor little book of mine is, frankly...

What is patriotism but the love of the good things we ate in our childhood?

Lin Yutang

Of course I despise my country from head to foot, but it makes me furious when a foreigner shares my feeling.

Alexander Pushkin

To live in a country without a sense of humour is unbearable; but it is even more unbearable in a country where you *need* a sense of humour.

Bertolt Brecht

For Fadia & Adel with faith in life & all my best

6.1.9?

Sections of this book originally appeared in the New Straits Times.
This book was sponsored by Maybank.
Skoob Books Publishing Ltd. gratefully acknowledges their assistance
and thank John S.H.Lee for his support.
Photographs © Mark Lovell

Introduction

Anybody who wants to understand cultural politics today should read this book. Anybody who wants to understand Malaysia today should read this book. And anybody who wants an insight into the confrontations of East and West, of Islam and the secular or Christian world, should read this book.

Salleh Ben Joned, poet and journalist, is an excellent guide through the minefields of misunderstanding that await the traveller at home or abroad. These articles and essays cover a wide range of issues, from the question of the National Language (and National Literature) of Malaysia to the death of Lorca, from the soporific dullness of hot Sunday afternoons in Kuala Lumpur to the Rushdie Affair, from erotic verse to the implications of the Fall of Granada in 1492. Salleh is a joker and a satirist, and he can make one laugh aloud, but beneath the wit and invective is a courageous seriousness. *Ridentem dicere verum quid vetat?* as Horace said - or "Who says I can't joke while telling the truth?". Salleh's jokes are often very near the bone, as are those of the best jesters, and he probably annoys his friends as often as his critics.

He writes in a political climate which is, to say the least, challenging. Malaysia should be grateful to him for communicating to outsiders so clearly and enjoyably its condition as it approaches the Millenium - though I don't suppose gratitude is what it always feels. After reading these essays, one has much more understanding of what is actually happening in a country whose relationship with Britain has recently been very vexed.

One can even pick up, from this volume, a few words of the language - it was Salleh himself in Kuala Lumpur who taught me the provenance of the word *amok*, and from these essays I have now learned that in Malay, breasts are *tetek*, a word which he lovingly describes as being completely expressive of itself, and more evocative than any English version, literary or vulgar. His translations of Malayan *pantuns,* sayings, and terms of abuse also make one long to know more of the language. It is clearly a fine tongue for invective.

Born in Malacca, Salleh had a Western education in Australia and Tasmania, and is now widely travelled, but he remains a Malaysian and a Muslim. He is uniquely well placed to explore what has recently become the dominant cultural conflict of our time. Like Rushdie, he has lived it, day by day, and tried to make sense of it. His responses are instant, off the cuff, sometimes hasty - and that is one of the virtues of this volume of occasional pieces. It has a great immediacy. The debate is with society, and he shows us a mind unable to censor itself. He explores the Qu'ran and the Hadith, finding there mercy and compassion: he challenges the dictators of religious orthodoxy on their own ground, pleading for a tolerance which he assures us has scriptural authority.

This is a brave agenda. The words "blasphemy" and "sacrilege" and "apostasy" understandably haunt him, and he says that his typewriter has a curious habit of producing the word "scared" instead of the word "sacred". His courage in trying to interpret one side of his heritage to the other, and hence to us, is exhilarating.

Salleh is bilingual, and writes in English and Malay: he supports strongly the right to write (and teach, and be taught) in English, but he also has a strong feeling for Malay. His games with words in both tongues reveal his knowledge of James Joyce, of whom he here writes with admiration - making, incidentally, some interesting comparisons between Irish nationalism and Malaysian nationalism. He is sensitive to the grey area where religion fades into nationalism, nationalism into power politics, and to the ways in which literature itself can be co-opted, abused and misinterpreted. He votes for multi-culturalism, but he understands its dangers.

Exhilarating, too, is the infectious enthusiasm with which he writes about writing. His friends and heroes, ranging from the Australian poet and trickster James McAuley to Octavio Paz, Ibsen, Chairil Anwar ("the first and probably the only true bohemian and rebel the Malay literary world has produced") and journalist and novelist Isako San, are celebrated with generosity.

Above all, he arouses our curiousity. He makes us want to understand. For this alone Malaysia should give him a few medals. Who would have thought I would find myself reading an article on the Bumi writers' dilemma with such interest? Until I came across Salleh Ben Joned, I never even knew what a Bumi writer was. This book challenges us all to find out.

Margaret Drabble
May 1994

MARGARET DRABBLE is a novelist and critic. Her first book, *A Summer Birdcage*, was published in 1962 to be followed by several others, including *The Millstone* (1966), *The Needle's Eye* (1972), and *The Radiant Way* (1987). She is editor of the Fifth Edition of the *Oxford Companion to English Literature* (1985) and is currently completing a critical biography of Angus Wilson to be published in 1995. She was awarded a CBE in 1980.

Preface

I have a small confession to make. I am not quite sure about this book, this possibly 'rancid' *rojak* (spicy Malay salad), of essays and a selection of newspaper columns. I had, and to a lesser extent still have, doubts about publishing it - if not the essays, then certainly the columns (aren't they too ephemeral, perhaps, or too 'Malaysian' to be worth reprinting for a wider audience?)

But my publisher and friend, Ike Ong, who for some strange reason, has an unshakable faith in the idea of this book (and in me too), rode roughshod over my finickiness and sudden seizures of cynicism (I *am* sometimes vulnerable to them), and simply bullied me into consenting to its publication. Ike Ong is a crazy man. Wonderfully crazy. His manic enthusiasm can be infectious. And for someone like me, can be quite dangerous. And liberating too. Yes, liberating.

So, Ike, you are as responsible for this book as I am. If it should find a fair audience and is considered to be really of some value, I'll of course swear eternal allegiance to you as my 'champion' of sorts. If it gets savaged - or even (perish the terrible thought!) pissed on ... well, remember, it's all your doing. Your bullying, your crazy enthusiasm. Cheers!

A word about my *New Straits Times* literary column, *As I Please* (AIP). The pieces, selected from a very uneven bunch, written, with lengthy annual breaks, over a period of three years (1991-1994) are presented here as they first appeared, with all their sense of topical fervour, urgency and the need to meet the deadline. Whatever minor cuts, insertions and changes in phrasing that have been made are dictated by the needs of the non-Malaysian reader. *AIP* kicked off on March 6, 1991 with a confident commitment to regularity. Quite soon it became 'As and *When* I Please' to the dismay of the papers' long suffering literary editor and the incredibly tolerant followers of the column. You see, I belong to the vanishing tribe of 'Old Malay' - which the currently much talked-about 'New Malay' would no doubt dismiss as lazy, irresponsible, cynical, indisciplined, unpredictable, fun-loving and therefore unreliable. I must be one of the most, if not the most, irregular, writers in the history of journalism. But this hopeless, so-called columnist, despite intermittent seizures of doubts about the quality of his writing, is sure of one thing. The column, if nothing else, triumphantly proved that one must never, never censor oneself, and that one should always, as they say, 'test the parameter'. Malaysian writers need to be reminded of this all the time - and I am sure the situation is not much better in many other so-called Third World countries.

Many people have expressed surprise that I was allowed to get away with saying the kind of things I said in *As I Please* in a country like Malaysia and in an establishment newspaper like the *New Straits Times*. The fact that an intelligent man and a Malay (it's worth noting), was chief editor of the paper explains the freedom I was tacitly granted. Not a few readers praised me for my so-called 'courage'; I personally didn't think it was a matter of courage. Commonsense - that's basically what's needed. That, and a real concern for the intellectual state of the country. I was furious when V. S. Naipaul, interviewed while in Malaysia researching for his book *Among the Believers*, so casually said that mine was "a country without a mind". But I knew what he meant, and if we confine that remark to the contemporary scene I couldn't help but agree with him.

I'm a stinking big-mouth, I know. But I really can't stand the provincialism of my fellow Malaysian, especially Malay (or Bumi) writers. The contemporary Malay writer *as a type* (which means there are exceptions) is an utterly predictable, cliché-clogged, slogan-sloshed, pretentious, sentimental, deadly solemn and therefore humourless animal. He takes himself so, so seriously - and for all his intellectual pretensions, he knows fuck-all about the big world. The Malay word for writer is *sasterawan* (Sanskrit in origin), and I must admit in my polemical usage the word has acquired a perjorative connotation. And thus the charge against me that I have blasphemed against the Holiest of Holies, the inbred figure of the Malay *sasterawan*, that shrill articulator of the Soul of the Race (race, not nation, mind you), that pious and sentimental defender of the glory of the Great Malay *Minda* (from the English 'mind' - you see, we don't even have a word for mind!). Blaspheming as I please against the *sasterawan* doesn't take much courage - and it can be fun. But I must admit my pieces on Salman Rushdie, especially the last one, (*Speaking up for a writer's right*, December 15, 1993) were a little reckless; my wife thought this time I was really asking for it. But Allah the All-Knowing, All Compassionate apparently didn't think I had committed any mortal sin (no lightening has struck me yet). There was, however, a flood of correspondence (one was ten pages long), all of it very fiery and very condemnatory, consigning me to hell with pious enthusiasm. The one from the Iranian Embassy Press Attaché came very near to demanding that I, a freelance writer, be "sacked" (sic) from the *New Straits Times* and be compelled to apologize to the government and people of Iran and the Muslim *Umma* (community) for insulting the memory of the Ayatollah. This letter was among those that were published before the correspondence on the subject was promptly closed by the Editor; but the paragraph containing the "demand" had unfortunately been edited out.

Writing a literary column in a country like Malaysia can be quite trying. The issues that matter keep recurring again and again, and when you want to be positive, to have the nice feeling of praising a writer or some writing for a change, there isn't very much to shout about. Thus my self-enforced soul-searching, soul-saving *khalwat* from the column every few months. The word *khalwat*, incidently, is of Arabic origin and it means 'spiritual retreat'. In Malaysia it has come to mean 'retreat for immoral purposes' or sexual 'close proximity', a crime-sin which is punishable by the shariah law (it only applies to Malay-Muslims - so much for the special rights and privileges of the Malay-Bumis).

This obscene, nay, blasphemous transformation of the word *khalwat* is a perfect figure for the general perversion of values, of the spirit, intellect, heart, life and inevitably language - all in the name of an abstract piety (in this case, religion; in another, race). If I were asked what motivates my writings, I'd say simply: the crying need to say "No! In thunder!" to this perversion. No, in the name of Yes-to-life. Yes!

Salleh Ben Joned
Aldie, Virginia, U.S.A.
22 May 1994

Essays

A Test to Pass

"It was my island too, my boyhood's home,
My 'land of similes' ... "
- A. D. Hope, *In Memoriam: J. P. M.,* 1976

Like many tipplers who have gone Downunder, when I think of Australia I immediately think of the pubs. How nice to be able to go back to one (though in the mind only - alas!) now that I feel the sudden urge to pay homage to one of my favourite Australian poets, James McAuley.

The pub I would like to go back to in this, my modest exercise in reminiscence, is not particularly distinguished by anything other than personal associations. It's in Hobart, Tasmania, which "was my island too" as well as McAuley's. It's solidly 'fair dinkum' - very Aussie, quite plebian and truly philistine. The poet whose name and work I am bringing into a most unlikely association with this pub happens to be one of the most uncompromising enemies of 'fair-dinkumnism' and philistinism Australian poetry has produced. Although in a sense, he is 'dinkum' poet ('dinkum' here means 'authentic') he is utterly contemptuous of the raucously self-conscious 'fair dinkum' tradition in Australian writing. You know, that 'temper-democratic-bias Australian' kind-of-thing.

The pub was called The Crescent. The name certainly didn't do justice to the gray grubby 'she's-alright-mate' suburban dive that it in reality was. The Crescent. Well, being a good Moslem, when I thought of the crescent, the Islamic paradise promised by the Prophet immediately came to mind. And I had a vision of paradisal rivers cascading with *aqua paradiso.* "Know that paradise is beneath the shadow of the sword." So goes one apocyraphal prophetic tradition; and paradisal swords are always crescent-shaped - at least to my mind.

Although I am not really nostalgic for the place, poetic justice demands that I go back to it. I wonder if it's still standing - there in that cheerless part of North Hobart. I remember well the oppressively salubrious air of suburban contentment; but I also remember equally well the splendour of the snow-capped Mt.

1

Wellington that dominates the old convict town, graced by the big beautiful River Dewent.

Tasmania - known as Van Diemen's Land in the old convict days - may be in Hal Porter's obscenely suggestive words in *The Tilted Cross*, "an ugly trinket suspended at the world's discredited rump." But to me the "ugly trinket" is what the "monotonous tribe" of "second-hand Europeans" of A.D. Hope's notorious poem 'Australia' have made of one of the world's most beautiful islands.

Tasmania - the island of majestic rivers, beautiful lakes with white sandy beaches (one of them, Lake Peddar, was drowned by the Hydro Electric Scheme during my time on the island), organ-piped mountains and impenetrable forests. The island is both part and not quite part of that huge hunk of a continent to its north, that "woman beyond her change of life, a breast/ Still tender but within the womb is dry." (A. D. Hope, *Australia*). This Tasmania had nurtured the boyhood imagination of Alec Derwent Hope, and matured into late lyric simplicity the poetry of James McAuley. Neither Hope nor McAuley was born in Tasmania, and yet that beautiful island was their "land of similes".

In a small unexpected way it was mine too. And I have a personal claim to the island as well as a 'poetic' one. Two of my daughters were born there; one of them is now part of the earth of the island, as much as Jim is. And it is appropriate in more ways than one that in Alec's elegy on Jim, that island of similes should be the ground and focus of meditation:

> This island which your lucid poet's eye
> Made living verse: wildflower and sedge and tree
> And creatures of its bushland, beach and sky
>   Took root in poetry,
>
> Until a world to which your poet's mouth
> Gave being and utterance, country of the heart,
> Land of the Holy Spirit in the South,
>   Become its counterpart.

How it came about that an innocent student from Malaya was transported to that unheard of place downunder - to study

English Literature of all things! - is a long story much of which is not pertinent to my present purpose. But there I was, dumped like a bewildered convict on the island of Van Dieman's Land, and made to serve hard labour for the unnatural term of my student life - all thanks to the well-organized mercies of the Colombo Plan.

And there was I in The Crescent one bitterly cold winter evening, drunk on Tasi's celebrated Cascade and the poetry of Alec Hope and Jim McAuley. What a combination! Goaded by my equally drunk mates, I had jumped on a bar stool and brazenly swilled the "pure sardonic draught" that had fecundated the satiric minds of Alec and Jim, the minds that have produced the notorious poems, *Australia* and *The True Discovery of Australia*. The first, which burst into print in 1939, had long become one of Alec's most scandalous poems. "Its reputation has pursued me like a bad smell", I remember Alec murmuring once. The second, a satirical narrative that takes off from Swift's *Gulliver's Travels* and published in Jim's first book, *Under Alderbaran* (1946), was not as notorious as Hope's poem; its notoriety was I believe eclipsed by another of Jim's sensational efforts of the Forties, the Ern Malley hoax.

The two poems were heady stuff to my adolescent mind. I can still feel the arrogant fervour with which I thundered and hissed those offensive lines into the astounded faces of the Crescent regulars - RSL diggers, honest clerks, good suburban chappies all. I wasn't merely reciting; I was drunk enough to dare mangle the lines by peppering my reading with my insufferable running commentary, squeezing salaciously sadistic pleasure out of such lines as these by Hope:

> And her five cities, like five teeming sores,
> Each drains her: a vast parasite robber state
> Where second-hand Europeans pullulate
> Timidly on the edge of alien shores.
> (Want to know what 'pullulate' means,
> cobber? Let me tell you ...")

That ringing verse modulating, in my drunken reading, into the quieter but no less brutal wit of Jim's:

Meanwhile, as you'd expect, their arts are poor
As if dust had leaked into their brains
And made a kind of dry-rot at the core.

Knowledge is regarded with suspicion.
Culture to them is a policeman's beat;
Who, having learnt to bully honest whores,
Is let out on the muses for a treat.

The Hope-McAuley picture of Australia was still basically true as late as the early sixties when I was a student there. Things, I'm glad to report, have changed since then, partly as the result of the 'uncringing' of the infamous Aussie 'cultural cringe' and the accompanying belated release of the Great South Land from the suffocating clutches of Victorian England. (The verses of Jim's I quoted above have, however, an applicability to our present situation here in Malaysia, where the mini Mullas and the mini Molochs - some of them calling themselves writers! - are threatening to bind us to an insane form of 'cultural cringe' fourteen centuries out of date).

My free recital at The Crescent, needless to say, was not appreciated. "Throw that bloody wog out!" (Or was it 'Abo', not 'Wog'? Because I remember I was often mistaken for an Aborigine; and Aborigines in those days were not permitted by law to darken the doors of Aussie pubs. No, not 'Abo', I think: that was in Adelaide where there were still a few of them left. In Tasmania there were none left, it being one of Tasi's claims to historic fame that its early White settlers successfully exterminated the entire native population of the island.)

And so I was bodily lifted by the burly hairy ape of a barman and thrown out into the street to lick my own chunder loo by the gutter. You see, I had not only insulted Australia Fair; I had done so in the lounge room of the pub (unforgivable - with all those genteel ladies present: women were not allowed in the bars in those days, Australians being very protective of the gentler sex). If the diggers had known that the obnoxious 'Abo' happened to be a beneficiary of Australia's Foreign Aid to Asia, they would probably have lynched this ungrateful Boong (another cute name for us Asiatics). It was bad enough that my

Aussie mates, long-haired 'hippie' ratbags some of them, had staged a walk-out in protest against my eviction. They too apparently never darkened the doors of the The Crescent again.

That incident, so predictable in its antipodian absurdity, coloured my long sojourn in Australia. That was how I first stained the innocence of that little corner of Australia's cultural backwater. That was how I sealed my passion for the best of McAuley's and Hope's poetry. And that was how my lasting ambivalent attachment to the Lucky Country began.

I went to Tasmania from Adelaide, and one of the reasons for the move was the presence of Jim McAuley as Professor of English at the University of Tasmania. Jim was lured into academia in 1961 at the rather late age of 44, after years of teaching a discipline totally unrelated to his vocation as poet. For fourteen years he was a lecturer at the Australian School of Pacific Administration, an experience that had no doubt taught him a lot about the realities of government and politics, and which must have influenced his notorious political conservatism of the late Forties and after; in the Thirties he was like many writers, more or less a radical. The period with A. S. P. A. was also significant for Jim's personal and poetic development: he formed a lasting attachment to Papua and New Guinea, and came under the decisive spiritual influence of the Archbishop of the Territory, Alain de Boismenu - both of which are beautifully celebrated in the poem *New Guinea*, included in his second book, *A Vision of Ceremony* (1956).

My tutor at Adelaide University, like Jim a Catholic convert, was an admirer of the poet-turned-academic. And when for personal reasons I was forced to make an escape from Adelaide, he suggested that since I seemed bent on learning all about poetry I should go to Tasmania and sit at the feet of the famous McAuley. I had wanted to go to Sydney, that Sodom Downunder - no doubt because of the bright red lights there - but I allowed myself to be persuaded by my tutor, though I must confess the name of James McAuley was then not at all familiar to me. To that god-forsaken island, whose existence I had barely heard of, I therefore went. It was like going to the South Pole I thought. But it was a decision I have never regretted.

The reason why my Adelaide tutor was so persausive was the existence of another 'poet' whom a group of Adelaide's angry young avant-garde literati had been hoaxed into publishing. The 'poet' was no other than the famous Ern Malley whose creator was none other than Jim McAuley. Jim, so he claimed, concocted in one beery afternoon Ern Malley's modernist masterpiece *The Darkening Ecliptic*; and, impersonating in a cute letter the dead 'poet's' sister, sent it to Max Harris of the noisy *Angry Penguins* (an avant-garde journal of the time published in Adelaide). Harris published it with the blessing of no less a person than the then formidable English poet-critic Herbert Read.

In the mad concoction of *The Darkening Ecliptic*, Jim was assisted by fellow poet Harold Stewart [1] - and, of course lots and lots of good Aussie beer, plus all kinds of stray publications that happened to be conveniently around, including, so legend has it, a U.S. Government Report on the extermination of Malarial mosquitoes! The Ern Malley hoax hit the international press - the first time, I suppose, an Aussie poet ever had that kind of luck; and the last too no doubt.

A man with that kind of reputation actually occupying the Chair of English in Tasmania - well, it was worth a try to sit at his feet, I thought; I might learn a few things. Learn I certainly did - and a lot too, but not without some resistence at first.

Like many young literary innocents, I had come to the University infected with vague utopian longings and an equally vague fascination with literary modernism. What the first year undergraduate didn't know when he made his *hijrah* (pilgrimage) to Tasmania was that James McAuley was an implacably sardonic opponent of both. The fact that the Ern Malley affair had dealt a cruel near-fatal blow to the avant-garde movement in Australia didn't really sink into my head; the idea that Jim was

---

[1] Harold Stewart, I last heard, had seemingly gone the way of Zen. Now apparently domiciled in Kyoto, he writes little poetic gems in the manner of the Japanese haiku. I sometimes wonder what the ghost of the Catholic McAuley thinks of his old fellow hoaxer in the garb of a Zen monk. But since Zen, with its love of zanny humour and outrageous practical jokes, is conducive to creative hoaxing, I imagine Jim is smiling a secret smile of understanding at his friend and fellow poet.

responsible for a hoax that had hit the headlines was more impressive and important to me.

I soon had serious doubts about Jim the political conservative with his stubborn 'reactionary' ideas, though I never made the mistake of thinking that he was some kind of reactionary hyena, or, to use that awful fashionable label actually flung at him on many occcasions, a 'fascist pig'. This was the violent sixties I am talking about, the era of Vietnam and campus revolt. Most of my close mates were New Left; one of my closest was actually a professional student in his late 40's dedicated to revolution who was maintained in one degree course after another by his hairdresser wife. None of these friends could understand why I thought highly of the 'fascist pig', and even liked him. Though I found Jim the political conservative insufferable at times, the literary conservative was something else. And my enormous respect for the man was not confined to literature, where, because of his anti-modernism, there were also serious differences of attitude. I also respected his political courage, his willingness to confront the anarchic rabble.

Just remember how many quite sober Professors in the sixties were cowed into spineless fashionable submission by the scruffy demagogues of the campus - and you will appreciate the moral courage and intellectual spine it takes to be a McAuley. Jim was anything but flabby; you could see his no-nonsense vigour in that strongly moulded face, the piercing eyes that stared at you from deep sockets, and that firm masculine walk of his that I thought so characteristic of the man. In spite of my vague 'leftish bias', he taught me to despise those flabby academic liberals and ritualistic radicals who, when it came to the crunch, didn't really know what they stood for; and so chose to swim with the tide, deluding themselves that they were for 'revolution', but utterly ignorant of the face of the beast. (Jim wrote a pointed little poem called *Liberal or Innocent by Definition* which all fashionable academic liberals and radicals should read.)

But it's Jim the teacher of literature and poet whom I want to recall in this essay in homage, though it is true that the public figure cannot be separated from the teacher and poet; in all the three roles he was distinguished by full-bodied convictions, by the firmness of his stand.

The fact that he was a practising poet and that he didn't become an academic by taking the usual route was one reason why he was such an unusual teacher. His approach to the teaching of literature (he mainly taught poetry) was refreshingly non-academic. His were the only lectures I never missed, and I was quite incorrigible in my belief that most lectures were a waste of time, preferring to spend my time in either the pub or the library. Quite the best part of Jim's lectures was his reading of the poems we were supposed to study. He had a wonderfully firm voice, sensitive and precise in placing and articulating the stress, alert to the subtleties of rhythm and pace.

I owe him a great debt in arousing and sustaining my appreciation of the resources of traditional metrics. He and Hope, obtusely and misleadingly dubbed 'neo-Augustan', are well-known in Australia as the most consistent and articulate defenders of traditional metrics. But reading their essays, incisive and revealing though they are, is nothing like listening to one of the practitioners himself demonstrating the virtues and unsuspected subtleties of a convention much taken for granted.

Jim may have been rather infuriating in his impatience with much of modern poetry; but the author of *The End of Modernity* certainly knew how to demonstrate the strengths and what he would claim was the indispensibility of the forms and intellectual-aesthetic assumptions of traditional verse. He never tired of stressing the importance of order and fidelity to the idea of "rational discourse" in poetry. Jim was a great enemy of the sloppy and the irrational, vices he associated with certain forms of self-indulgent romanticism. But that doesn't mean his notion of poetic discourse was narrowly 'classical' or 'rational'. To get some idea of what he meant by poetry as 'rational discourse', one has only to read that early poem addressed to the well-known critic and friend, the late Vincent Buckley:

> Scorn then to darken and contract
> The landscape of the heart
> By individual, arbitrary
> And self-expressive art.

Let your speech be ordered wholly
By an intellectual love;
Elucidate the carnal maze
With clear light from above.

Give every image space and air
To grow, or as bird to fly;
So shall one grain of mustard-seed
Quite over-spread the sky.

Let your literal figures shine
With pure transparency:
Not in opaque but limpid wells
Lie truth and mystery.

It is worth comparing this poem, *An Art of Poetry*, to an even earlier poem, *The Muse*, which is addressed to Alec Hope. It is to be noted that Jim's commitment to rational discourse or poetic lucidity was informed by a sense of the mystery at the heart of things, as well by the need, desperate in an age so irrational as ours, to cling to hard-won ideas of intellectual and spiritual order. He would say: it is no way to understand the human condition or to celebrate life by surrendering to the forces of the irrational - both in matters of ideology and poetic form. Let us, he would say, be sober in our drunkeness with both the blessings and the terrors of existence:

Living is thirst for joy:
That is what art rehearses.
Let sober drunkeness give
Its splendour to your verses.
(*To Any Poet*)

The voice of the poet must not be the willfully idiosyncratic voice of the self-conscious individual intoxicated with his own oddity:

Compose the mingling thoughts that crowd
Upon me to a lucid line;

Teach me at last to speak aloud
In words that are no longer mine.
(*Invocation*)

I cannot over-stress the gifts that Jim offered his students in this matter of understanding what the craft of poetry - poetry in traditional forms at least - is all about. His sense of the value of order and lucidity informed his teaching in a variety of ways. When he found how atrociously impossible the hand-writing of his students was, he actually spent an entire lecture, complete with demonstration, on the art of hand-writing. (He himself had a beautifully crafted style.) When he discovered how ignorant even Third Year students were about metre and scansion, he immediately gave a series of lectures on the difficult subject. These lectures, lucid and revealing in the best McAuley manner, were later published in book form: *A Premier of English Versification* (separately published in the U. S. A. as *Versification: A Short Introduction*). Jim McAuley on metre is to me only equalled by the American critic and poet Yvor Winters. Jim and Winters had quite a few things in common; both were implacable enemies of the shoddy and the irrationally obscurantist. I remember Jim urging me to read Winter's *Forms of Discovery* as soon as it came out by showing the draft of a review he had written of it.

What I now understand of traditional metrics I owe almost entirely to Jim, a knowledge that helped me to understand what he was fighting for in his own poetry, and Alec in his. It's a great pity that many of my leftish fellow students who read poetry didn't warm to Jim's verse, not a few of them dismissing it as 'academic' or 'old-fashioned'. I suspected that the reason for their lack of enthusiasm was their simple inability to *hear* the poetry. Somehow the voice of James McAuley the intransigent idealogue and 'Cold War warrior' got in the way of their hearing, even of the non-political poems, which actually constitute the bulk of his *Collected Poems*. I suppose the same reason accounts for the fact that, as Vivian Smith, poet and critic, puts it in his monograph on Jim, "of the six most important modern Australian poets ... McAuley is the most reluctantly admired."

Jim's unusual virtues as a teacher were not only revealed in his unconventional professionalism and clear-headed distrust of

10

bullshit of all kinds; they were also revealed in that passionate commitedness of his to definite viewpoints and the willingness to say so in no uncertain terms. A qualification is perhaps required here: Jim's passionate commitment to strongly-held views on literature and politics never in my experience made him forget the unspoken contract between the teacher and his students. In the public sphere he was a relentless and dedicated 'propagandist', but never in the classroom. As he himself said in an interview he gave me as editor for the campus newspaper: "I find it difficult to formulate a clear code of academic conduct in this matter. The nearest I can get to is to say that the academic has the ordinary rights as a citizen to be politically active, but he also has the professional duty to teach honestly and treat his students with complete fairness, and to respect their opinions. I hope I would be as much opposed to a right wing lecturer polluting the academic process as I am to a left wing lecturer doing so. Total objectivity can't exist. One can only hope that one's students do recognise that one is trying to be honest. I think most students like to feel that their teachers are capable of having definite views." (*Togatus*, Vol. 40, no. 9, 1969).

Jim's other striking virtue as a teacher was that, though he could be a terror with his piercing eye (especially if you came late to his lectures and walked right into the middle of his reading), he never kept his distance with his students. It was one of the pleasures of my student days that every time we students threw a party and invited him, he seldom failed to come; and when he came he really came to enjoy himself. Often he would stay until the early hours of the morning, telling us amusing anecdotes or giving impromptu lectures on Solzhenitsyn, say, who was of course a must, or on some insufferable cult figure like Herbert Marcuse, who would of course be dismissed as a dangerous crank. Sometimes he would be drunk, but quite pleasantly - and I must say he was even better as a teacher then, for alcohol only made him more recklessly lucid and sharp.

He was an incredibly busy man; it's amazing that he could find time for us students, to drink and be merry with us in fraternal unselfconscious abandon, totally unrestrained by his professional status. It might be thought that there is nothing so extraordinary about this. But I teach at a university which is governed by ancient, almost feudal, notions about the proper relationship between lecturers and students; it's a pleasure therefore to recall those wonderful unstuffy days in remote Tasmania.

Yes, Jim McAuley was a remarkable, and to me even a great man, and a very unusual teacher. When I heard of his death late in 1976, I was in Denmark, uncertain of my own future and full of doubts about my profession as a university teacher of literature. I remember going out to walk across the snow-covered field behind my father-in-law's place, soon after reading the letter that brought me the news of Jim's death. As I sat down on the snow under a bare elm tree in that desolate part of Jutland so mercilessly exposed to the inscrutable sullen sky ("Here everything lies naked and uncovered before God" - Kierkegaard), I thought of my teacher and of the poet I was privileged to have known. A number of well-remembered poems, a few from *Under Aldebaran* but mostly from my favourite volume, *Surprises of the Sun* (1969), came naturally to my mind. The ones from the latter volume came blazing, resonant with well-remembered echoes of his precise subtly-cadenced voice.

That volume contains the poems that Jim suddenly came to write in the late sixties; they are poems about his childhood and youth in an emotionally and spiritually deprived home in a Western suburb of Sydney, about his school-teaching days in the mining and industrial town of Newcastle, and about his marriage in 1942. These 'confessional' pieces were a bit of a surprise because of Jim's long-standing distrust of that mode of poetry, a mode that requires more than the usual tact because of its ego-centred tendencies and proneness to self-indulgence. I remember him being hard on Robert Lowell for what he considered his typically American kind of confessional perversity; when I hazarded the guess that Lowell had probably unconsciouly influenced his decision to write his own 'confessional' poems, his answer was a gritty denial.

To many people, myself included, *Surprises of the Sun* was indeed full of surprises. In some ways the book was a welcome departure from the 'predictable' style and preoccupations of his middle consciously Catholic phase. Perhaps 'departure' is not the right word here; for it can be argued that the poems in that book are, stylistically at least, the proper final fruits of his long poetic endeavour. The vein of lyric simplicity, so pronounced in *Surprises of the Sun*, had in fact been with him from the beginning; it could be felt even beneath the more formal, ceremonial or discursive language of his middle phase.

The poems that came to my mind as I mourned the death of my teacher, there in remote Jutland, were not all great stuff. But every one of them was special to me then; they were more immediately meaningful because of the difficult situation I was in at the time.

Stray lines came through the freezing wintry air like true surprises of the Winter sun. Some of them had the simplicity of colloquial statements made truly felt and memorable by the full context of the poems, the well-remembered music and tones. Jim, in his last phase, really had this facility of making simple statements about hard simple truths that are almost epigrammatic in force; the well-cadenced lyric mode in which such statements are realized explains the force. I think Jim had, more often than not in his last phase, realized his "persistent desire to write poems that are lucid and mysterious, gracefully simple but full of secrets, faithful to the little one knows and the much one has to feel." (Introduction to his own selection of his poems in the book he edited, *A Map of Australian Verse*.)

It was no effort for me then, without his books around in Jutland in December, 1976, to recall such lines as these:

> Some like me are slow to learn:
> What's plain can be mysterious still.
> Feelings alter, fade, return,
>
> But love stands constant in the will:
> It's not alone the touching, seeing,
> It's how to mean the other's being.
> (*One Thing At Least*)

The much-loved poignant poem about his parents, *Because*, I could remember in its entirety. Although I never had the bad luck to have a father like Jim's ("My father had damned up his Irish blood/Against all drinking praying fecklessness/and stiffened into stone and creaking wood./His lips would make a switching sound,/ as though spontaneous impulse must be kept at bay.") - although I never had his bad luck, the poem spoke to me then quite directly:

13

the complex re-enacted feelings it tries to come to terms with are not of the sort confined to parent-son relationships, and are therefore something one could empathize with. And the stark honesty of its perceptions, so painfully wrung from a past that still haunts, is compelling because it's deeply felt and realized with poetic tact and precision and resource; prose-like but made taut by concealed bindings.

> I never gave enough, and I am sorry;
> But we were all closed in the same defeat.

> People do what they can; they were good people,
> They cared for us and loved us. Once they stood
> Tall in my childhood as the school, the steeple.
> How can I judge without ingratitude?

> Judgement is simply trying to reject
> A part of what we are because it hurts.

But the poem that really made me question myself as I lay "naked and uncovered before God" under that bare elm tree in Jutland was *Self Portrait, Newcastle 1942*, which I must be permitted to quote in full. The last but final verse, I remember, sent a sharp chill down my spine, even more than the re-enacted terrors of the middle verses:

> First day, by the open window,
> He sits at a table to write,
> And watches the coal-dust settle
> Black on the paper's white.

> Years of breathing this grime
> Show black in the lungs of the dead
> When autopsies are done;
> So at least it is said.

> Sunset over the steelworks
> Bleeds a long rubric of war;

He thinks he knows, but doesn't,
The black print of the score.

He, like that sullied paper,
Has acquired no meaning yet.
He goes for long walks at night,
Or drinks with people he's met.

In sleeping panic he shatters
The glass of a window-pane.
What will he do with his life?
Jump three storeys down in the rain?

Something - guilt, tension, or outrage -
Keeps coming in nightmare shape.
Screams often startle the house:
He leaps up blind to escape.

By day he teaches the dullest
Intermediate class;
He gets on well with them, knowing
He too has to test to pass.

With friends he talks anarchism,
The philosophical kind,
But *Brief an einen jungen
Dichter* speaks close to his mind.

Terrors and loneliness, both from the past and in the present, doubts and pretense, were all faced with non-defeatist, gently ironic honesty. And "deeply submissive/To the grammar of existence,/The syntax of the real" (*Credo*), the poet knew too that life must be accepted as a gift to be celebrated in poetry with joy. The beautiful landscape of Tasmania, his "island of similes", gave him frequent moments of epiphanic joy. The spare, firmly sensuous, deceptively flat but syntactically well-structured short poem *In The Huon Valley* is an example of such moments of epiphany. I quote only the second and third verses:

Juices grow rich with sun.
These autumn days are still:
The glassy river reflects
Elm-gold up the hill,

And big white plumes of rushes.
Life is full of returns;
It isn't true that one never
Profits, never learns.

His faith in his God gave him strength to confront the complexities and contradictions of existence; but that faith was never easy with him, as is generally assumed, especially in the last phase of his poetic career. Not with the man who could say, in reference to Milton's belief about the role of evil in the world, that he had "no talent for comprehending the thoughts of God. The mystery of evil remains terribly dark to me, even in the light of faith." The sense of the terrible inscrutability of evil - evil inherent in the human condition, not merely social and political evils - is strong in some of Jim McAuley's poems. See, for example, that terrifying narrative *A Leaf of Sage*.

And it was no surprise to me to discover that one of his very last poems should be this very moving farewell to life:

So the word has come at last:
The argument of arms is past.
Fully tested I've been found
Fit to join the underground.

No worse age has ever been -
Murderous, lying, and obscene;
Devils worked while gods connived:
Somehow the human has survived.

Why the horrors must be so
I never could pretend to know:
It isn't I, dear Lord, who can
Justify your ways to man.

Soon I'll understand it all
Or cease to wonder: so my small
Spark will blaze intensely bright,
Or go out in an endless night.

Welcome now to bread and wine:
Creature comfort, heavenly sign.
Winter will grow dark and cold
Before the wattle turns to gold.

Explicit (Quadrant, December, '76)

"No worse age has ever been" - yes, true perhaps; but equally true is Jim's full-bodied commitment to the present, the now, "Yes now, in the deepening spaces of the dusk" (*Spring Song*). Another often repeated assumption about Jim is that he was besotted with the past. This assumption is grossly simplistic. Tradition was very important to him, yes, but

Not if it means to turn
Regretful from the raw
Instant and its vow.

The past is not my law:
Queer, comical, or stern,
Our privilege is now.

St John's Park, New Town

It is the same spirit that dictated his editorial for the inaugural issue of *Quadrant*: "In spite of all that can be said against our age, what a moment it is to be alive in!"

Yes, how the man loved life and the moment he was privileged to live in. I remember one occasion when Jim's sheer lust for living was memorably revealed to me. It was in 1970 I think, the year of his first serious illness that less than six years later was to kill him. He had just been discharged from St Mary's Hospital; and looked horribly emaciated. Though he had been instructed to stay at home to recuperate, he insisted on joining a group of students on a week-

17

end skiing trip up Mt. Field in Southern Tasmania. We went in his yellow-and-white Holden station wagon, with him driving. I remember, before we left, his wife, Norma, telling him: "Now, don't you stay up all night talking to your students." But that of course was exactly what he did. After tramping around in the snow all day (he didn't or couldn't ski), in the evening in the ski lodge he performed in his usual McAuley manner, not as if he had just survived a very serious operation. He was up all night long. One by one we dropped off to sleep, leaving Jim and one entranced girl student by the fire. At about 5 a.m. I woke up, and heard him, with one arm around the girl's shoulders (paternally of course), murmuring into the smouldering fire: " ... the heart of man is savage ... and lonely ... ". And marvellously sturdy too, I should add. His certainly was. Lonely, savage, sturdy - and capable of much generosity and gentleness.

February, 1984

The Art of Pissing
An Open Letter to Redza Piyadasa

Introductory Note

The incident that is the subject of this open letter to one of the
most vocal artists and art critics in Malyasia occurred in 1974.
The setting was an exhibition frighteningly called *Towards a
Mystical Reality* held at Sudut Penulis (Writers Corner) of the
Dewan Bahasa dan Pustaka. It consisted of 'found objects' (a half-
empty Coca Cola bottle, a dirty abandoned raincoat found on some
rubbish heap, a half-burnt mosquito coil and that sort of thing). It
was accompanied by a manic manifesto full of abstractions, capital
letters and exclamation marks.

There were about fifty people - artists, writers and students - in
that corner to witness my little gesture of friendly protest. The
incident went unreported in the press; I was told that somebody
or other had managed to have it hushed up, and I, having made a
public exhibition of myself in that hallowed corner, was not about
to make another one in the media.

The incident would have remained a lost footnote in the history
of modern Malaysian art if, about a year later, Redza Piyadasa
(bless his soul) had not challenged the perpetrator (*individu* was
the word he used) of this sacrilegious act to explain "the rationale"
of that act. This challenge occurred in the course of a debate in
Dewan Sastera on the direction of modern Malaysian art between
Piyadasa, Siti Zainon Ismail and one or two others. It was a
challenge I had been waiting for.

My open letter was published uncut, title and all, in the July
1975 issue of *Dewan Sastera*. For this I have Usman Awang,
then editor of the magazine, to thank. There was some faint
resistence to certain parts of the letter at first, and I remember
having to argue quite vociferously in defence of the title I had
chosen (*Kencing dan Kesenian* or *Pissing and Art*). But Usman as
editor was a true gentleman who was willing to listen to
argument.

I don't know what my *kurang ajar* (ill mannered) act was worth, if it was worth anything, from the point of view of the history of Malaysian art. This is for our art historians to judge. I note that the distinguished art historian T. K. Sabapathy has a flattering comment on my letter, and even quotes from it in his Introduction to *Modern Artists of Malaysia* (1983) which he co-authored with Piyadasa. But from Sabapathy's comments you wouldn't know anything about the incident that provoked the open letter he refers to. I sometimes wonder what the silence here means.

What is the point of reprinting this letter? Am I not content that the incident has passed into the folklore of Kuala Lumpur underground; and that I have, by the simple act of unzipping my trousers and zipping up my mouth, attained minor Malaysian immortality? (I must admit that some inherited perversity makes me rather fond of the smell of the past; and the 'Mystical Reality Incident' has certainly pursued me, to echo the words of an Australian poet about a notorious poem of his published in his youth, like a familiar bad smell?)

Yes, what's the point? Well, I would say that the points raised in the letter have more than topical relevance. If asked to sum up its significance in one sentence, I'd say it defends what I see as the true values of art and intelligence against the pretentious, the false and the fashionable. And the target of the letter is an artist of no mean standing in this country whose 'Mystical Reality' thing - both manifesto and exhibition - is considered by Sabapathy a significant event in the history of Malaysian art.

As for the pissing act itself, I still consider it, to put it in the language of Asian courtesy and modesty, as much a 'breakthrough' in the history of modern Malaysian art as the exhibition called *Towards a Mystical Reality*.

> A dunce once searched for a fire with a
> lighted lantern.
> Had he known what fire was,
> He could have cooked his rice much sooner.

- from *The Gateless Gate* by Ekai
(translated by Paul Reps)

Dear Piya,

Whenever I open my big mouth, people say vulgarities and obscenities pour out.

When I unzip my trousers, they say I sully my self-respect.

That Salleh fellow, is he ever "serious"? Pissing, being vulgar and obscene - that's the only thing he's good at. How disappointing when one thinks of "our Eastern values". Blah, blah, blah ...

Alright, Piya, this time I'll be a good Easterner - and you I hope will be a good listener. I accept your challenge that "the individual" who *"membuang air"* (literally "threw away water", i.e. urinated) at your exhibition, *Towards a Mystical Reality*, should come forward to "explain the rationale of his act". Actually I've been waiting for quite some time for this opportunity to explain an act that a lot of people seemed to have completely misunderstood; to set out my real attitude to your exhibition and to the manifesto that accompanied it.

Let me begin with two observations which don't really require much elaboration, and two admissions which will be explained and defended later.

First observation: Our artists (that includes writers) and intellectuals tend to be on the whole a solemn lot. They tend to confuse solemnity with seriousness, verbosity with intellectual breadth, and pomposity with depth. This tendency often goes with egotism and an embarrassingly acute sense of their own impor-tance. And need-

---

[1]   By "our contemporary cultural life" I mean mainly the world of letters, and Malay world of letters at that. "Malay" because I refuse to pretend that there is a national cultural life in this country, simply because there is no such thing, at least not yet, as a truly national culture.

less to say (this being Malaysia, it has to be said of course), it also goes with shallowness of mind.

The most noticeable thing about our contemporary cultural life is the relative absence of humour in the field of ideas.[1] Oh, people make jokes of course, and usually of crudest variety. They even attempt what they call comedy and, God help us, even satire. That's not what I have in mind. The humour I mean is bound up with a balanced conception of the intellectual and artistic life; it implies the capacity to distance oneself from what one is doing, to see things, including oneself and what one is doing from different, usually unfamiliar points of view. This capacity Malaysian (predominantly Malay) men of letters and intellectuals are not distinguished with. That's one of the things that make our intellectual life dreary and dry. Satire and parody are conspicuous by their absence, at least as a viable tradition (the existence of isolated attempts at such forms only serves to prove my point). In such an arid intellectual landscape, to expect the solemn Malaysian (again, Malay) Artist (with a capital A, a connotation better suggested by the contemporary usage of the Malay word *seniman*) - to expect this animal to laugh at himself is like expecting the dew to drop at midday.[2]

Second observation: The two major categories of people in the world of the arts in Malaysia are the type who says yes without understanding and the type who says no equally without understanding. Most of those people who welcomed or rejected your manifesto and your exhibition, Piya, belong to these two categories.

Now I would like to make two admissions. First: What I did at your exhibition was actually a serious act; serious but not solemn, and contained elements of the purposefully playful. The act was carefully thought out, and had a clear rationale. Second (this will probably make people think I am not right in the head, or incorrigibly facetious even when I protest the earnestness of my intention): Not only was my action fundamentally serious, it was also consistent with the spirit of Zen which you keep invoking in your manifesto!

---

[2] Literal translation of the Malay saying *harapkan titik embun di tengah hari*

Yes, there *was* an unashamed stink of Zen in my pissing, Piya. ("Stink of Zen", by the way, is not a gratuitously rude expression but a fairly respectable phrase often used in Zen literature.) If the atmosphere that surrounded the opening of your exhibition had been different, and the people there were not as solemn as they were or not so awed by the self-declared importance of the occasion, they would have smelt the stink of Zen and laughed the laughter of Zen. You will remember that although the target of my 'Zenny' gesture (a Westerner schooled in the antics of Dadaism would probably have called it 'Dadaish') was the whole idea of the show, my actual pissing was aimed at a specific object. Not one of those 'found objects' that constituted the so-called exhibition, but the only object that was not 'found', that was created - the manifesto itself. At the moment the piss hit a copy of the manifesto a loud laughter should have been heard from among the audience - the laugher of enlightenment, at least with regards to the meaning of the gesture. R. H. Blyth says of Zen's deliberate use of humour: "Laughter is breaking through the intellectual barrier; at the moment of laughter something is understood." (*Oriental Humour*)

You and I, Piya, have often argued, at times heatedly. Not infrequently the argument is mere noise; there is no real dialogue. Because you are extremely vocal, even eloquent, and fond of abstractions, you tend to talk at people, not to them. Most of us, especially the manic among us, are often guilty of this vice. But you, I think, are more guilty than most.

Nonetheless, despite all the sound and fury, sometimes the points of your opponent do get through to you. At least at the level of the unconscious. I would like to think that this was the case when I argued against your manifesto the day you came to my house with a copy hot from the press. I said, didn't I, that if you went ahead with the exhibition I would shit on it? You heard it, but couldn't believe what you heard, or that I would really do it. (Thank God for everybody concerned that the threat could only be partially realised; our bodies don't always do as we want them to.)

I don't suppose you can remember what you registered of my argument that day. Well, let me repeat it.

Basically, Piya, I do respect the *intention* of your manifesto and exhibition. I respect your commitment to art and the life of the intellect. You rightly feel that something vital is missing from our

23

cultural life, and something should be done about it. "Respect" did I say? But ... there is always a 'but' to my yes, Piya. (Well, not always; but often - especially when it comes to matters of ideas.) The proof of my respect is that I actually read your manifesto, really read it - with a red pencil in my hand. It was no fun, I can assure you, because the thing is quite unreadable.

I sympathise with your intention of creating a habit of polemic that is positive and dynamic (how you love the words 'polemic' and 'dynamic'). There are a number of things in your manifesto which are relevant to our situation, though I can't really say there is anything in it which is truly new. I support in particular your appeal to our artists and writers that they should be more aware of the rich cultural and philosophical traditions of Asia and their relevance to the perennial needs of man. (It is ironical that this Asia-centric business was got going by Westerners; and there is a danger that it will become a mere fad, if it hasn't already become one, as it has in the West.)

I also agree with you that many of our artists (and writers) "are not aware of the implications of the idiom (idioms?) of modernism they use in their works". But this doesn't mean I agree with your call that they should all be as articulate as you are in matters of theory and in polemics. I don't see any reason why *all* painters must be expected to theorize or engage in polemics. If a painter like Latiff Mohidin, for example, is content with just painting, he should be left alone to do what he does best. It's good enough they are articulate on canvas without having to be articulate on the typewriter as well. But if they can, of course we would like them to be so.

I appreciated your intention, but I wasn't happy with the tone, the manner and certain other things about both the manifesto and the exhibition. My little act of protest was a gesture that was clear in motivation, but not without ambiguity. A number of factors provoked me to do it. I won't deny the mischievous side of me had a hand in it; the exhibitionist in me too no doubt. But believe me these were not decisive factors. Do you really think I would *melacurkan maruah* (sully myself or prostitute my self-respect) just for a joke? You've got to be joking, Piya.

24

Among the major things the act set out to do was to test a central premise of your manifesto, as well as to protest against what I saw as pretentious, contradictory, and false.

I was prepared to do this although I was quite conscious of the risk I was taking. Among the risks was the likelihood of the act being completely misunderstood, seen as an anti-intellectual buffoonery, perhaps even hooliganism. I was prepared to take the risk in the name of commonsense and for the sake of genuine intellectuality and true spiritual values.

There is an element of 'bullying' in the rhetoric of your manifesto - a juvenile sort of 'bullying', and pretty embarassing in its excess of self-consciousness and solemn protestations. "OUR ART WE ALSO DECIDED WOULD BE MYSTICAL IN NATURE!" Who are you trying to convince or impress, Piya, with your capital letters and exclamation marks? Yourself? Those who have some idea of true mystical insight might just wonder if you know what you are talking about; they might feel "mystical" is not something one or one's art can just *decide* to be.

If the "mystical" is understood as a direct translogical knowledge or experience of the divine, the transcendant, or the 'oceanic', I wonder how you, prisoner of verbalism that you are, can ever be a guide to us? Listen to this: "... modern art ... finding its raison d'être in a dialectical reconsideration of phenomenal processes ..." Often this sort of 'rhetorical *amok*' is repeated, capital letters and exclamation marks bandied around so indiscriminately, almost threateningly. You claim in the Forward that you have undertaken a "voracious reading programme" (it had to be "voracious" of course) lasting two whole years specifically for this manifesto. I am impressed, and prepared to believe that you know the meaning of the words you use with so much relish. But, as I suggested above, a Zen master would most probably be amused by your "raison d'être", your "dialectical reconsideration", etc etc.

Well, Piya, you with your 'Zen', I with mine. In a way it was Zen which inspired my zippy comment on your "dialectical reconsideration of phenomenal processes". I can't really say I knew what kind of reaction to expect. Shock from the majority of those present obviously; even arrest for indecent exposure. But, against my better knowledge of Malaysians in such situations,

I vaguely expected at least one or two people to burst out laughing. No one did. (One person, however, did walk up to me and touch my shoulder, which I took to be a gesture of solidarity.)

I must say I was a trifle disappointed by the total absence of even a smile. I don't know what sort of Zen books you have been reading, but the ones I've read are full of humour, even accounts of practical jokes. These Zen jokes are designed to shock the Zen aspirants into awareness; they also affirm what I've always believed in - that in a philosophy that sees life as a unity, the mundane and the mystical, the sacred and the profane merge; ordinary categories that separate reality and experience into compartments are ignored. Zen as I understand it is also always alert to signs of falsity, quick to mock anything that forgets reality in the name of Reality.

I can recall a host of anecdotes from Zen literature that demonstrate this. The story of the Buddha and his flower sermon you yourself must have come across in your voracious reading programme. You must also have read some of those stories that climax with the kick of the Master on the monk's backside that produces enlightenment, or with the Patriarch tearing a sacred manuscript into shreds and tossing it into the winds. Of the anecdotes that are 'vulgar', my favourite is the one that was made the subject of a painting by the eighteenth-century Zen painter, Fugai Mototaka. The story tells of a Zen monk on a very cold day burning an image of the Buddha to warm his backside. When reprimanded by a fellow monk, who was shocked by the act of sacrilege, the first monk said (tongue in cheek) that he was burning the image to obtain *sarira* (an indestructible substance found only in the ashes of cremated saints). He could find no *sarira* from the ashes of the image; therefore it couldn't have been a saint's, and since the day was even colder than he had thought, the monk went on to burn two other images to keep himself warm.

So, Piya, like the flower sermon of the Buddha, like the kick of the Zen Master that produced enlightenment in the earnest seeker, and like the burning of the image of the saint to warm one's bum on a cold wintry day, my *kurang ajar* act at the opening of your exhibition was designed to shock you into enlightenment about some homely truths concerning art and reality. What could be more concrete, more ordinary and at the same time "mystical" in the sense of revealing "the essence of phenomenal processes" than the processes of our own body such as pissing and shitting that we do everyday (at least I do; I don't know about you)? So, from this point of view, my act of spontaneous theatre had the aim of testing one of the major premises of your manifesto and exhibition. This, as well as protesting against the false, the pretentious and the contradictory in it.

The atmosphere of the opening was such that it could not have induced the state of meditation that you claimed to have wanted in order to bring your audience into "confrontation" with the essentially "mystical" nature of reality.

In your manifesto you go on about "the self-effacing role of the artist". This may be evident in the objects of the exhibition, and consistent with your shrill rejection of the concept of art as expression of the artist's personality. But the nature and tone of your manifesto, and the manner and atmosphere of the exhibition clearly contradict your claim to a "self-effacing role". No, Piya, you are not a self-effacing invisible *dalang* (the unseen puppeteer in Malay shadow play); you are a modern artist like all modern artists, subject to all the usual pressures and needs.

It wasn't supposed to be an exhibition; it was supposed to be an "experience", a "direct confrontation with (mystical) reality". But it still had to be legitimised by the presence of a representative of officialdom; and he of course had to give one of those usual speeches. What did you say, Piya? A situation conducive to meditation on "mystical reality"? Were you serious, Piya?

The aim of the whole endeavour, however misguided, could only have been saved by something unexpected, by something that proved its essential point, however clouded by confusion and pretension, virtually in the teeth of its arrogance. That act of mine was something unexpected. So, Piya, you should have been thankful to me for pissing on your sacred text that morning in Sudut Penulis.

John Cage whom you seem to admire would certainly have appreciated my gesture. Cage, also influenced by Zen, at least has got the essential message of that incredible philosophy, and is never solemn. The critic Virgil Thomson, an admirer of Cage, once described a Cage concert in New York in 1958 as "cartoon comedy". One recalls Marcel Duchamp, the one-time Dadaist, saying, "Humour is a thing of great dignity."

Our local 'guru' of the performing arts, theatre critic Krishen Jit, who is so dazzled by your rhetoric, affirms your proud claim to be (together with your collaborator, Sulaiman Esa) "savage innocents". Sorry Piya, innocent you certainly are, but "savage"? - far from it. Innocent in the way you get so terribly excited, like a kid with new toys, over newly discovered notions that are already dated elsewhere; but far from savage in your understanding and ability to deal with reality (with a small r).

Actually, Piya, your concept of art seems to me to be ambivalent, if not confused. Your manifesto suggests that what you set out to do in the exhibition wasn't 'art' ("direct confrontation with reality"), but also 'art' (thus words like "We are approaching art ... "). If your aim was to bring us into "direct confrontation with reality" (why "confrontation" and not simply "experience", say?), I in my simplicity of mind would like to ask, if that is your aim, why talk about 'art' at all? If you really don't want to have anything to do with art, have the guts to say so. In that case, you needn't have dragged all those so-called 'found objects' into Sudut Penulis. It seems you are not that certain you don't want to have anything to do with 'art'; you still want to cling to the word, however supposedly radical your concept of art may be.

What exactly is your function, Piya? If I want to experience reality directly, to meditate on the "mystical" dimension behind ordinary objects and experiences, why shouldn't I do it on my own, free from manic manifestos, free from boring speeches by cultural bureaucrats - in short free from the Piyadasas of this world? Why on earth should I "buy experience" from you? ("The person buying my work will really be buying an actual experience not an artifact," says Redza Piyadasa!)

I remember Jasper Johns saying: "What makes something art is it being placed in the context of art." My agreement with Johns hangs on that "something". Context is important, tradition is important, the complex of intellectual assumptions is important; that's why anti-art only works by reference to art. But not everything that is dragged into the context of art and draped in custom-made theory can be considered 'art'.

I don't agree with Cage (whom you follow so slavishly) that art and reality/life are the same. Art is 'based' on reality, perhaps even 'feeds' on reality; but art and reality are not identical. If we truly value reality/life, we cannot possibly confuse the two. But art can deepen and widen our consciousness of a reality that is multi-dimensional. To perform this function art needs form; but it must be stressed that the concept of form meant here is not static or rigid. The important thing to realize is that art cannot run away from form. The literary and art critic Harold Rosenberg once reminded artists and writers, "Formlessness is simply another look, and a temporary one at that. In time, organization shows through the most chaotic surface."

Piya, Piya! You want art, but how confused you are about what art is. You want reality, but how innocent you are about reality. Reality? Just remember the rainbow arc of my piss, the fountain of life that affirms and celebrates the unity of reality: the vulgar and the refined, the bawdy and the spiritual, the concrete and the transcendent, the stinking and the mystical, the profane and the sacred. A zippy gesture of affirmation that you would do well to meditate on.

So, my dear Piya, (and Cik Siti Zainon too), when I unzipped my pants at the opening of that historic exhibition, I wasn't "prostituting my self-respect". I was just revealing reality.

Fraternally yours,
Salleh

A Little Knowledge is Not *Always* a Dangerous Thing:
Kassim Ahmad and the Hadith

Introductory Note

This piece was written at the height of the controversy on Kassim's book on the Hadith in 1986. Given my problematic relation to the subject, it was rather brave of me to dare to enter the debate. And because this is Malaysia, it was also quite reckless. But I was saved from my own recklessness by the banning of the book. In this country when a book is banned all discussions on it are also 'banned' (not officially but by the operation of self-censorship by editors). I personally have never been good at self-censorship, and the habit of recklessness simply refuses to go away despite advancing age. The inclusion of the following article in this book is, I suppose, another testimony to my love of exposing myself.

In publishing his little book *The Hadith: A Re-evaluation*, Kassim Ahmad has become the first 'fool' in this country to rush into a territory where even angels fear to tread. The territory is a treacherous theological thicket ruled with monopolistic rigour by a secret society of *ulamas*. The sign at the entrance says: LAYMEN, KEEP OUT! And in red: Or be damned as a *murtad* (apostate).

Many of the things Kassim says in his book are old hat in some Muslim countries - Eygpt for example, where from the time of Muhammad 'Abduh in the late 19th century a lively debate on the Hadith has been going on. But this is Malaysia, and I take my sullied *ketayap* off to Kassim for his initiative and courage. Apparently he had been advised, nay warned, that his thesis was ill-founded and dangerous because subversive of the 'unity of the *umma*' (community of believers). But he persisted, especially after the lectures on which the book is based and which were originally scheduled to be delivered at the UKM, were torpedoed. For his stubbornness I again take my *ketayap* off to him (I like stubborn people).

30

Taking off *ketayaps* again and again can be boring, and when I read the spirited piece by another stubborn 'fool' in support of Kassim (Ghani Ismail, *Totalitarianism versus Hadith New Straits Times*, June 12), I decided to be a fool myself and join in the fray. May Allah the All Merciful help me! My knowledge is very little; but with all due respect to the Professor from the International Islamic University (see *New Sunday Times*, June 22), a little knowledge is not *always* or *necessarily* a dangerous thing. The knowledge may be little, in the sense of not being comprehensive or specialized, but may be enough to grasp the essentials of the issue. And the issue here is too important to leave to the *ulamas* or the academics, genuinely expert or otherwise.

What *is* the issue? In the immediate sense it concerns the authenticity and relevance of the Hadith. On the question of authenticity I happen to have some opinions, but I dare not say them too loudly. I have read a few books, but, not knowing Arabic, and having to depend mainly on infidel scholarship, I feel vulnerable. And the predictable bogey of 'Orientalism' which they are using to scare off Kassim, does unnerve me a little. Especially when one of the orientalists whose scholarly book on the Hadith I find most revealing and persuasive happens to be a Jew (I refer to the great Hungarian scholar Ibnaz Golziher). In our country they are so omniscient that they see the long arms of Zionism everywhere. (It's bad enough to be damned a *murtad*; but a *murtad* who is also a Zionist stooge is destined for the seventh pit of hell.) It is no use pointing out that the Jew in this case is a scholar respected by the Arabs and that some of his writings have been translated into Arabic, and are actually used for teaching Muslim Arabs their own religious heritage.

What about the question of relevance? Authentic or not, should the Hadith (which is the work of man) continue to be the source of Islamic theology and jurisprudence, second only to the *Quran* (which is the Word of Allah)? I have been advised not to open my big mouth on this too. Not only am I a mere layman, but a disinherited one too, cursed by both ignorance of the language of Revelation and the misfortune of being Western educated. But since some important principles are involved here, more fundamental than the issue of authenticity and relevance, I think I'll stick my neck out - and be damned with it.

31

My basic sympathy with Kassim is prompted by a number of things. Even if he is wrong on certain matters (which has yet to be proved), he has, by publishing his book, let in much-needed fresh air into the closeted in-bred world of Islam in this country. (I should add, to prevent misunderstanding, that Islam itself is not closeted; but the suspicion of the intellect on the part of our *ulamas* makes it appear so). Kassim's book is a reassertion of the Muslim's right, a right rooted in the *Quran*, to use his God-given mind - or to borrow the language of Islamic jurisprudence, the right to *ijtihad* (individual judgement).[1]

The tyranny of *taqlid* (imitation, or blind acceptance of authority) had immobilized the minds of Malaysian Muslims for far too long. I learn (not from an orientalist this time) that the word *taglid* literally means a necklace or something worn around the neck. This literal meaning certainly suggests submissiveness and mental slavery.

Frankly I sometimes envy those simple-minded souls to whom faith is a simple matter of doing what their *lebai* or *imam* says. But it's too late in the day for modern educated Muslims to yearn for the cosy security of their grandfathers. The great Muslim theologian and mystic, Al Ghazali, in his spiritual autobiography, *Deliverance From Error*, says: "There is certainly no point in trying to return to the level of naive and derivative belief (*taglid*) once it has been left, since a condition of being at such a level is that one should not know one is there; when a man comes to know that, the glass of his naive beliefs is broken. This is a breakage which cannot be mended ... The glass must be melted once again in the furnace of a new start, and out of it another fresh vessel formed." (Translation by W. Montgomery Watt.)

It seems that what Kassim and other like-minded Muslims before him are trying to do as far as the foundations of the Shari'a (Islamic law) are concerned is nothing less than to melt Islamic law and theology once again in the furnace of a new start. Since most of the Hadiths are spurious, and since even the genuine ones are culture-

---

[1] *Ijtihad* is here used in a non-technical sense - i.e. I am claiming the right to *ijtihad* for every Moslem in possession of a sound mind and a sound education. I see no reason why the exercise of your God-given mind in this area should be the monopoly of the *ulamas* and the *mujtahid* (religious scholars).

bound and limited by the historical circumstances and humanity of the Prophet, Kassim argues that they ought to be abandoned as a source of Islamic law (law and theology are, by the way, inseparable in Islam). The *Quran*, with which many injunctions of the Hadith are in conflict, should, Kassim further asserts, be the only guide for Muslims.

Now, this is quite a radical proposition whose implications are truly far reaching - more than Kassim seems to realize. His dream of wanting to rid Islamic law and theology of all the anomalous elements in it has my sympathy. But I have the feeling that the realization of that dream might involve more than he bargains for. Go back to the *Quran*, and only the *Quran*, he says, and we'll recover the pure faith and pristine simplicity of Islam - as well as justice and brotherhood. But can it be as simple as that? It seems so to Kassim, as the flawed logic in his argument suggests.

He claims for example, that since the establishment of the dubious Hadith as a source of theology and jurisprudence was the main cause of the break-up of the Islamic world that led eventually to the decay of a great civilization, its abandonment would ensure the recovery of the lost unity and greatness. I find his argument here rather simplistic, however much I share his hopes.

He reminds us that many hadiths were most probably invented by interested factions to further and justify their political causes. This hadith-mongering had led to the increase or intensification of dissension in the Islamic world. But since dissensions were already there before those hadiths were invented, they could hardly be blamed for what was bound to happen anyway. If they had not invented hadiths, they would have resorted to divergent inter-pretations of the *Quran* itself to validate their factional interests. Kassim, rather simple-mindedly, thinks that just because the *Quran* teaches the principles of truth, brotherhood, justice and all that, going back to the Holy Book as the source will solve all problems. The *Quran* may be clear about many things, but it can also be very opaque or at the very least ambiguous (I am judging on the basis of translations, of course, and of what scholars, both Moslem and non-Moslem, say about the language and style of this extra-ordinary book).

Take the Quranic verses on apostasy, a subject close to my heart. Some notable Islamic scholars claim that these verses do not give justification to the law that apostasy is a crime that merits any punishment, least of all the death penalty; it is a sin punishable in the hereafter, yes, but not a crime punishable by the state. But these same verses (for example verses 11-12 in Surah *Taubah*, or 54 and 57 in Surah *Al-Mai'dah* and *Al-Azhab*) have been used to argue the opposite. Those who have so argued buttressed their interpretation with the appropriate hadiths of course.

Kassim also argues that even if the Hadith and the Sunnah (practice of the Prophet) were authentic, Muslims should not be bound by them. The Prophet was after all a human being conditioned by the circumstances and the needs of his time and his culture. What is of universal application is not what the Prophet was alleged to have said or done, but what he conveyed to man in the form of the *Quran*. Kassim's distinction between Muhammad as Prophet and Muhammad as a man and political leader seems on the surface valid. But my little knowledge of Islamic theology and metaphysics tells me that the idea of prophethood precludes such a distinction. Muhammad may have been a man - a fact which is stressed frequently, true; but his humanity is imbued, so Muslims believe, with the light of prophecy. This makes his nature and function more than normally human, without however negating the human dimension and without compromising the idea of the absolute oneness or unity of God (*tauhid*). (The notion is lucidly explained by two writers on Islam I much admire, one a Muslim and the other a Swiss Orientalist - Syed Hossein Nasr and Frithjof Schuon.)

The hadiths, the authentic and the non-authentic, have the function of crystalizing, among other things, the metaphysics of prophethood. A modern secular scholar would say that they serve the functions of a 'myth'. The 'myth' (in the modern specialized sense) of Muhammad as Prophet is, I think, essential to Islam. If you dismantle that not much would be left - other than moral platitudes which all religions teach. (Though, it should be said, in Islam these platitudes are given more weight by a concrete philosophy of action - at least in certain areas concerning the governing of society.)

There is a lot that is frankly antediluvian and innane in the Hadith; I am with Kassim here. Some of the Hadith-based laws which are obviously bad - the ones on apostasy and the position of women, for example - could and should be reformed or dropped. They appear to be in conflict with the *Quran* anyway. But the Hadith also contains some wonderful things, some of them sheer poetry to my disinherited mind. I know Kassim doesn't recommend that the whole lot be jetisoned, contrary to what his detractors claim. (Kassim's careless polemical language and manner of argument is partly to be blamed for this misunderstanding.) But, he asserts, the authentic and worthwhile Hadiths that can be retained are not binding. They cannot have the force of the *Quran* because they are historically bound. Since, as I understand it, the Hadith and the Sunnah constitute the foundation of the 'myth' of the Prophet - a myth validated by what can be taken as implicit in the *Quran*, and since where myths are concerned the question of factual truth or otherwise is irrelevant, Kassim's view contains implications more radical than he seems to be aware of. I dread to speculate on those implications.

Whatever it is, the problem is very complicated. Enlightened Muslims must find it difficult to deny themselves their right to exercise *ijtihad*; liberate themselves from the tyranny of *taqlid* and the *ijma* (consensus of *Ulama*). They will want to invoke (whether they are anti-Hadith or not) that marvellous saying attributed to the Prophet: "The difference of opinion among the learned of my community are a sign of God's grace." But if they exercise that right *to ijtihad*, they must be prepared for the consequence. To borrow the language of Al-Ghazali, the inherited mental glass cries to be melted in the furnace of reason. But reason can be a treacherous thing; that was why Al-Ghazali himself turned to mysticism.

But since not all of us have the qualities of a mystic, we have to turn to poor reason - and, hopefully, the imagination too.

Meanwhile, we must learn to be wary of the Muslim who, when cornered in an argument, resorts unthinkingly to the Hadith. If I myself were caught with such a Moslem, I would deal with him in the spirit of the famous humorist of the early 8th Century, Ash'ab. Ash'ab said something very witty and to the point when he was taunted for his apparent frivolity by a Hadith-besotted fellow Arab. I quote from Ibn Qutayba, *Uyan al-Akhbar*:

"Someone said to Ash'ab: If you were to relate traditions (Hadith) and stop telling jokes, you would be doing a nobler thing."

"By God," answered Ash'ab. "I have heard traditions and related them."

"Then tell us," said the man.

"I heard from Nafi," said Ash'ab, "on the authority of Ibn 'Umar, that the Prophet of God, may God bless and save him, said "There are two qualities, such that whoever has them is among God's elect."

"That is a fine tradition," said the man. "What are these two qualities?"

"Nafi forgot one and I have forgotten the other," said Ash'ab. [2]

June 23, 1986

---

[2] See *Islam: from the Prophet Muhammad to the Capture of Constantinople*, Vol.II, Edited and Translated by Bernard Lewis (New York, 1974)

Is Nothing Sacred?
Or Down by the Salleh Gardens
(An ABC of Reading Poetry for Local Professors/Academic
Critics as Well as an Advertisement for Myself)

There is no doubt that Salleh Ben Joned, whose first collection
of poems did not find a publisher until he was in his mid-forties,
is an anomaly - a Malay anomaly. Salleh's anomaly is multi-
dimensional, and this he has tried to suggest in the Malay title of
his bi-lingual book - *Sajak-Sajak Saleh*.

The pun on 'Saleh' is obvious of course, but it is not the only
pun - Salleh's *Sajaks* or Poems [1] and, if a translinguistic pun is
permitted, 'Sullied Poems'. (If you want to involve a third
language, there is the French *sale* hovering somewhere behind the
English 'sully'.) The 'sullied' is for the benefit of those Malay critics
and writers who are excessively conscious of the bogey of 'ethnic
purity' in poetry. They will read all kinds of 'impurities' into Salleh's
stuff and no doubt conclude that the guy is beyond redemption,
from the point of view of ethnicity at least. These poems are not
the works of a *Melayu* (Malay); only a writer whose sensibility
has been sullied by undesirable foreign matter could have written
them. In other words these are poems of a *Mat Saleh*, i.e. an *Orang
Putih* (White Man), specifically a Britisher, albeit *celup* (not authentic). (God knows why Brits are called *Mat Saleh*!)

For those *Melayus* who are also self-conscious about being Moslem (that means the overwhelming majority), an added help would
be in order. (This is afterall an ABC of reading for them, isn't it?)
These readers will have concluded from what they have heard of

---

[1] *Sajak* means rhymes, verse. It also means handsome, as in *pemuda yang
sajak* (handsome youth); or fitting, appropriate, as in *mendapat isteri
yang sajak* (found a fitting wife). I personally prefer *sajak* to *puisi*, but I
can see there is a case for using both words. *Sajak* can be used to mean
rhyming verse (without the connotation of lightness which the English
word sometimes carries), and *puisi* to mean what its English original,
'poetry', suggests - something more comprehensive, embracing both free
verse and poetic prose as well as rhyming and blank verse.

37

Salleh Ben Joned ('Ben' is of course a clear sign of his secret Zionist, therefore anti-Islamic, sympathies) that the purity of his religious identity is also questionable. They will be glad to be informed that the pun of 'sully' on Salleh/Saleh is an unconscious acknowledgement of this, for 'sully' is from Latin *suculus* which is a diminutive of *sus*, a boar or swine. See, I can be very helpful.

Salleh or Saleh (one or two 'l's is immaterial, I think) as a common Malay name is Arabic in origin (there was a prophet long before Muhammad named Salih). The name means 'pious', which is of course very appropriate for a prophet; but in the case of our poet … well, I don't know.

Perhaps Salleh, acutely conscious of being alienated from the Malay cultural tradition as it is currently or popularly understood, would like to make a claim to a heritage that goes further back in time, perhaps into prehistory, long before the race was saved by the coming of Islam. Perhaps he wants people to be aware of the 'Malay meaning' of *saleh*, not the Arabic. For *saleh*, according to Marsden and Wilkinson, means 'distinct, particular'. Winstedt, who is more alert to the variety of regional usage, has more to offer. His *Malay-English Dictionary* gives the following meanings: 1. (Kedah) throwbacks - of animals, fruits; freak - e.g. albino 2. (Penang) motion to or from as in *saleh kemari* (be pleased to come here); *saleh kembali* (revert). The third meaning reverts to that of the original Arabic: pious.

I think one should be constantly aware of the 'Malay meaning' of *saleh* when reading Salleh's poems. (I can hear an academic voice objecting: "That so-called 'Malay meaning' was an invention of colonial Orientalists, and therefore *tak boleh palai* (unacceptable)." Really, Prof? Are you sure you know your sources? In any case, the meaning is endorsed by no less an acceptable authority than *Kamus Dewan*, Prof.)

So *saleh* is 'distinct', 'particular', 'odd' 'individual', 'freakish' (I particularly like that 'albino' bit). An individual who 'comes and goes', and who is an 'throwback' to some lost ancestral form.

Now we know why Salleh's book got the reception it did. The book, apparently, was found to be so 'shocking' (*dasyat* was the word often heard) that it left the usually vociferous (and highly shockable) Malay critics almost mute with disbelief. There was not a single review of the book in the Malay papers or literary magazines. This is not really surprising in a society which often prefers to deal with the uncommon or the unabsorbable by pretending it doesn't exist. The book, however, did get a reponse, generally favourable, from the English reading public; all the reviews that appeared were in English.

This Malay anomaly called Salleh Ben Joned recently received the attention of a leading Malay literary figure, the academic poet professor Muhammed Haji Salleh. In a special poetry number of the journal *Tenggara* (24/89), of which he is co-editor, the Professsor has three articles. One of them is a survey of contemporary Malay poetry accompanied by a selection of recent stuff in translation. Salleh Ben Joned in one of the poets dealt with in that survey.

As far as Salleh knows, this is the first time that his poetry is discussed by a Malay academic critic. Salleh does not quite know whether he should be grateful for this unexpected attention. The uncertainty is quite understandable. The professor's comments on his poetry are frankly quite obtuse, but under the circumstances even an obtuse reaction from such a quarter, he feels, may be better than no reaction at all. Perhaps. Salleh is really not quite sure.

I must admit if there was a Malay academic critic who could be expected to deal with Salleh's works with a fairly informed mind, that critic would be Professor Muhammad Hj Salleh. Considering his educational background, formal qualifications, exposure to literatures other than Malay and Indonesian, he should not be part of the tribe of ethnocentric *katak di bawah tempurung* (frogs under a coconut shell), the kind of *kataks* given the *ketok* (knocks) of ironic mockery in the opening paragraphs of this piece.

But something has obviously happened to the professor since he decided to embark on the programme of 'recovering' his *Melayuness*. Now that he occupies the Chair of Malay Literature at the National University, the need to assert his *Melayuness* is even stronger, especially in the face of attacks by jealous *kataks* who dare to question his right to pontificate about Malay aesthetics and arbitrate on the relative worth of Malay writers and works, classic or contemporary.

This must account for the professor's strange reaction to Salleh' book. Confronted with Salleh's self-proclaimed sacred and profane stuff (note the invisible hyphens in the 'Sacred and Profane' of the title, as they were by the alert Adibah Amin in her review of the book in the *New Straits Times*, August 14 1987), Professor Muhammad's critical faculties, nay, even his very ability to read poetry, seems to have deserted him. He admits that the appearance of Salleh's book was "the most traumatic of experiences" for "the Malaysian literary scene". ('Traumatic', mind you! To be quite honest, Salleh was rather pleased with that word, for never in his wildest dreams did he imagine that poetry - least of all his - could have such an effect.)

Trauma aside, Professor Muhammad takes particular exception to Salleh's blatant refusal to assume the stance of "the poet as a leader and elder of society." No, thank you, Prof ... Salleh feels that it is this business of the poet as leader, *solemnly and self-consciously assumed*, that is in part responsible for the typical Malay poet being a bloody bore. Salleh for his part gets easily embarrassed and feels he would be made barely articulate by the suffocating mantle of the elder of society. Especially when he feels (in spirit at least) forever young, younger in fact the older he gets.

Salleh wants to be heard of course, distinctly even if at times ambiguously. He wants the ambiguity (not something much valued here) to be distinctly registered, especially when there is a risk of him being considered for one of those literary prizes on the committee of which our professor may be sitting.

So, traumatised apparently by Salleh's 'peculiar' approach to poetry writing, and puzzled by his reluctance to play the part of elder and leader, and also shocked obviously by his plain-speaking about certain matters, our earnest professor could only react the way the typical Malay reader or critic would react. After mumbling about 'trauma', 'sacrilege', etc., he categorically asserts that to Salleh "nothing is sacred, neither family nor religion nor the moralistic myths."

The word 'nothing' *can* be dangerous when used so categorically. Afterall, even nothing *is* nothing. Even the blasphemous Earl of Rochester, the notorious 17th century poet and rake, admitted nothing "hath a being ere the world was made." You ponder hard on that line, and you will realise that this kind of nothing is not just nothing. Some of Salleh's poems on religious themes can be said to affirm this paradox. Even 'nothing' is sacred to Salleh. Disinherited Salleh's mind may be, but certainly not secularised. In fact he is quite 'scared' of the sacred to make nothing of it. (It's symptomatic that everytime he wants to say 'sacred', 'scared' gets typed.)

To buttress his assertion of the anti-sacred or non-sacred tendencies in Salleh's poetry, our traumatised professor could only and helplessly resort to the convenient clichés of his trade. Clichés which are easy substitutes for hard thinking and hard feeling, and which are much resorted to by Malay literary critics. 'Rebel', 'outsider', 'sacrilege', and of course the inevitable *kurang ajar* (rude and untutored) are bandied about as if they were nothing. And the professor of course takes several paragraphs to say the damned nothing (i.e. his 'nothing', not mine), and in awkward English too. And in the process he manages to make the reader suffer the hilariously painful sight of the mangling of Salleh's Malay poems in his deadening English translations.

The professor (quite surprising this, considering his reputed familiarity with world poetry and poetics in English) simply cannot read poetry except in the manner sanctioned by the established habits of his Malay-educated fellow critics. For example, he cannot make the elementary distinction between the voice in the poem and the writing person behind the voice, between the person of the poet and his persona, between the 'scandalous' autobiographical elements and their poetic transformations.

What 'scandalous' autobiographical elements? Oh, well ... you know, those ... those 'personal sexual act (sic) with women' (with women, mind you!) that Salleh is supposed to have re-enacted shamelessly in his salacious stuff; all the scandalous things he says about his dead father (imagine making the dying father hiss 'bloody bastard!' with his last breath!), his wives (infidel wives too), and his daughters. One of the daughters he claims to be proud of, and even dedicates the book to her. Yet, for some perversed reasons known only to himself, he could write a lengthy light verse that seems to make unkind fun of the poor girl!

The poem that Professor Muhammad focuses on in his discussion of the "scandalous autobiographical elements" in Salleh's work is *Dendang Si Tegang Pulang* (The Salacious Rhymes of the Self-taut Prodigal). His reading of the three-part poem is not only literal but earnestly one-dimensional,showing no sensitivity to its formal and rhetorical strategy as well as its tone. Because of this, he is not aware that the poem is in part of a mocking illusion to his own *Pulang Si*

41

Tenggang (The Return of Si Tenggang). The allusion is direct only in a few places - especially in the title and in the phrases *sopan santun* (courteous) and *Melayu jati* (true Malay) in the first and third parts of the poem; but the whole of the *Dendang Si Tegang Pulang* could be read as in part a 'parody' of Muhammad's *Tenggang* poem.

Like Muhammad's poem, Salleh's too alludes to the legend of *Si Tenggang*, the archetypal prodigal son who forgot that paradise lies at the feet of mothers - or the shores of the Mother Country; but the allusion is mocking and ironic, as the punning variation on the name suggests (*Tenggang/Tegang*). Salleh's *Si Tegang* (*tegang* literally means 'tense', 'taut', 'erect') is, as the professor for once accurately comments, a voice very much "on heat". Propelled by the swinging beats of its syllabics, the poem mockingly echoes the Muhammad Hj Salleh-type English-educated poet's defensive postures and predictable thinking about identity. Among other things, it says that if you believe and feel in your liver that you are still essentially a Malay after all the cross-cultural wanderings and acts of miscegenation (literal or metaphorical), then you *are* one. No need to make a self-conscious or defensive noise about it, saying, as Muhammad does in his poem, that "I am still a Malay, still courteous", and saying it in lines that are not only deadly solemn but embarassingly self-congratulatory ("I am still a courteous person, you know.")

I would say that a Malay poet's 'Malayness', to the extent that the thing matters in poetry, must be allowed to speak for itself while the poetry is busy on other things. Damn those chauvinistic critics who question what you in your liver knows to be the case, and pity those insecure poets and professors who are self-consciously defensive about cultural identity. In any case, a distinction has to be made between essential and formal or official Malayness. And even that 'essentail Malayness', whatever it is, does not have to remain completely pure, if that is possible, for a Malay poet to remain Malay. If your 'Malayness' is somewhat sullied, so what? So much the better if it means you are a fuller human being open to the sheer variety and richness of life. The purity of a poet's identity, cultural or racial, is not necessarily important to the business of writing poetry. All that writing poetry requires here is honesty, skill, clarity of mind and heart. That, and a sensitivity to the furious rumblings in your ancestral gut, the kind of sensitivity suggested by the aphorism that Lin Yutang once memorably and shamelessly burped: "What is patriotism but the love of the good things we ate in our childhood?"

May 1990

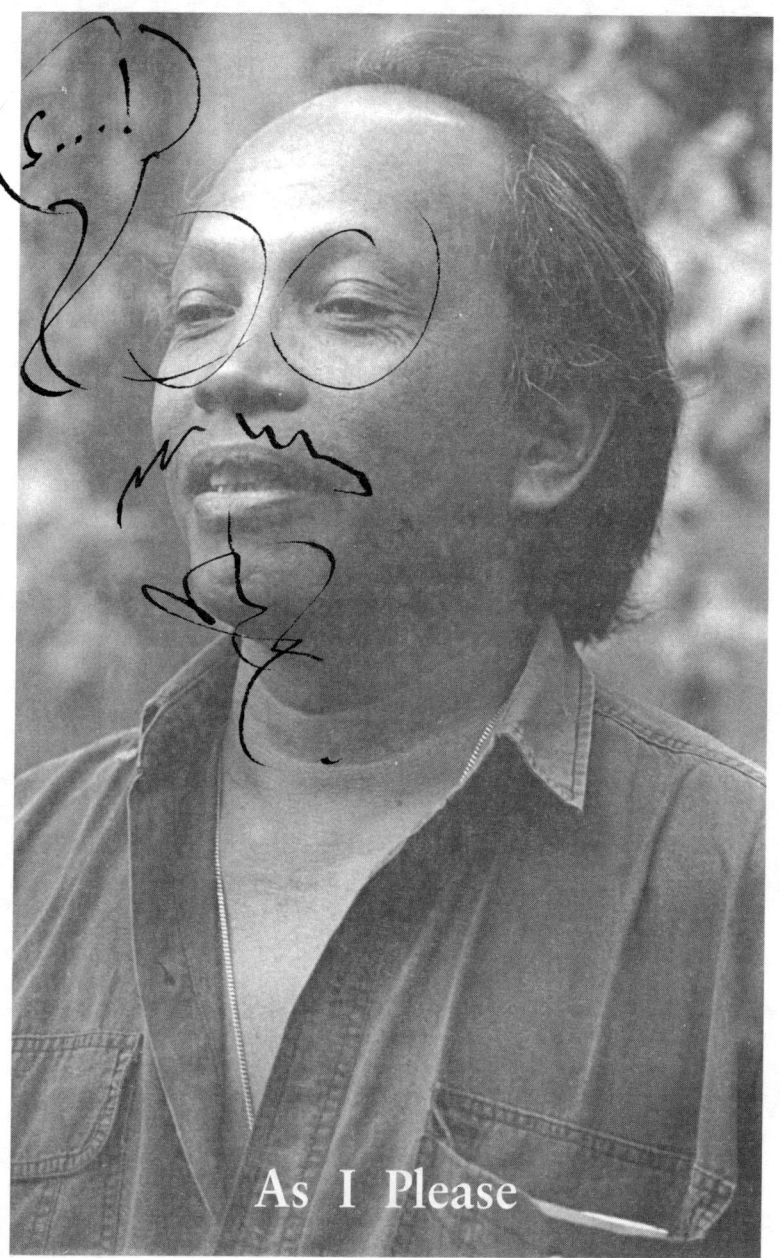

As I Please

The (Malay) Malaysian Writer's Dilemma

[1st January 1992]

An intelligent and morally sensitive Malaysian of Malay origin to whom self-respect and the dream of the brotherhood of man are as vital as the air he breathes is not an enviable creature in the age of NEP (New Economic Policy). The Government's attempt to get his fellow Malays out of the 'Malay dilemma' has put him in a new one - the Bumi Dilemma. *Bumi* is short for *Bumiputera*, literally, 'son' or 'prince' of the soil, i.e. the Malays and other natives. It can be a somewhat prejorative term, at least when used by non-Bumis especially in the post NEP era.

The 'Bumi Dilemma' afflicts only a tiny minority among the *Bumiputeras*. Under certain circumstances, or at its most acute, it can be in some ways almost Hamlet-like in its neurosis. To be or not to be part of a 'protected species': that is the question. Whether it is nobler in the mind to 'opt out' for the sake of necessary pride and independence and fidelity to ideals that transcend barriers of ethnicity - that, or to commit some kind of moral suicide by accepting unquestioningly those convenient pieties about ethnic survival and dominance. The Bumi afflicted with this dilemma may accept the rationale of the NEP as a time-bound historical necessity. And he may be able to see and acknowledge how, like other similar good-intentioned 'correctional' policies, it can be abused. He may even be willing to admit that, though he as an individual doesn't need the protection of such policies, directly or indirectly, whether he likes it or not, he is a beneficiary. But, because of the kind of individual he is, the situation he can find himself in as a result of being a member of a 'protected species' is not an enviable one. It is especially unenviable if he is a writer.

As I see it, the most serious problem for the Malaysian writer of Malay origin has to do with the question of fidelity or loyalty. And this question, because of its peculiar implications and of the pressure of certain stubborn ethnic realities, raises the question of a proper audience for the writer. The phrase "Malaysian writer of Malay origin" is here used after some thought; unwieldy though

47

it is, I can't think of a better one to stress certain realities and remind ourselves of what is supposed to be our common dream. As I have suggested above, the 'Malaysian writer of Malay origin' that I mean here refers to a tiny, very tiny minority within a much bigger group. The majority of this group can't be bothered with fine semantic distinctions between 'Malaysian writer of Malay origin' and simply 'Malay writer'. In fact, it's a matter of pride and ideological principle with many of them that the latter is used without question, just as they hardly ever question the givens of ethnicity and religion that make an innocent term like 'Malay writer' bristling with divisive connotations. And what is truly, chillingly disturbing is that these givens seem to be becoming more and more set, more shrill. The shrillness is the most immediately disturbing; it's the shrillness of ideological atavism that, I believe, is death to the creative principle.

The vast majority of Malaysian writers of Malay origin are, I believe, untroubled in any serious way by the question of audience. They just know who constitutes their audience, and they don't have the slightest doubts about it. One sometimes gets the feeling that they deeply believe and rather like it that things will remain unchanged, the solidity of their audience guaranteed, written into the Constitution as it were, which, in a sense it is. Similarly, the question of aesthetic, intellectual and moral fidelity doesn't trouble them. Fidelity to them is mainly a question of being true to certain ethnic pieties; truths and ideals not narrowed by the myopia of race and religion don't concern too many of them. The best way to make the problem of audience and the issue of loyalty something that could be concretely felt is for me to talk about it from my own personal experience.

I feel, in fact, I know in my blood and my bone that I belong to the tiny minority. Every time I sit down to write, I am bugged by these troubling questions: who am I writing for, in actual fact and ideally speaking? What am I supposed to be loyal to? In my pessimistic moments, I even wonder if I have any audience to write for; if the element of stubbornness in my notion of loyalty and fidelity had not condemned me to a no man's land. It's quite easy for my conscious self, the self moved by the will and governed by intelligence, rationality and ideals of common humanity, to say that as a writer I recognise only one loyalty: loyalty to truth and beauty, justice and freedom as I perceive them with all the honesty I could muster, with an informed mind and an informed heart.

But in this country, 'loyalty' is a very difficult business. And if, like me, you happen to be a writer somewhat alienated by your education from the dominant values of your ethnic kind, a writer who stubbornly persists in trying to see through and beyond the inherited blinkers of race and religion, what you call 'loyalty to truth and beauty, justice and freedom' can be considered a betrayal. And for the Malays, this 'betrayal' is a form of apostasy. People like me, bilingual and untroubled by sentimental pieties, are particularly vulnerable to the damning charge of 'apostasy' - apostasy from the religion of race, which can be a worse charge than apostasy from the religion of the race.

When I came back to Malaysia after a decade in a foreign country, I made a conscious attempt to recover my lost cultural self. Being a man of words, the attempt naturally took the form of repossessing my mother tongue. But, as everyone who has gone through it knows, such attempts can at best be only partially successful. So was mine - and I don't regret it. Quite frankly, I didn't want to recover my original cultural identity in its fullness and purity. The idea of recovering something of the 'purity' of Malay language itself might appeal to the poet in me, but not those values whose 'purity' or 'Malayness' cannot be distinguished from atavism. I am aware that I am in some ways quite Westernised, and I am not embarrassed by it. In fact, there are elements in my Westernisation that I am quite happy about, which I'd like to believe have made me a better human being and hopefully a better writer. But I also feel I am still, in some things, incorrigibly Malay. And I don't regret that either. In fact, there are things about 'Malayness' (not to be confused with 'Bumiputeraness') and in the cultural heritage of my race that I am terribly proud of. That's why I like Lin Yutang's unusual definition of patriotism (or eating, it doesn't really matter which) as love for the good things one ate in one's childhood. I am quite certain that these things, in my case *sambal belacan* (Malay delicacy) and *cincalok* (Malay delicacy), both literal and metaphorical, inform my writing, especially the poetry. Directly or indirectly, they give much of whatever energy my writing can claim to have.

Because this energy is inevitably life-affirming, its source cannot be 'exclusively Malay'. The streams that water my being, my life, my dreams, my writings are many and various, though the central one is no doubt Malay. I am a human being as much as I am a Malay Malaysian; Malaysia is my country and so is the world. Actually, my true country is not the world, but world literature. I am told that in Tagalog, a cousin of Malay, the word *Malaya* means freedom or consciousness. Well, that's the 'Malaya' I love to inhabit and feel terribly loyal to, a country that has no border with that other one - the country called World Literature.

An Austrian friend once gave me a poetry book called *Song of Malaya* by Ugandan poet Okot p'Bitek. No it's not about our country; it's about a prostitute, for the word *malaya* means that in Swahili. When I get depressed or angry because of the atavistic fantasy of 'Malaya' and 'Melayu' befogging the already blinkered minds of our *sasterawans* (writers), I think with bitter cynicism of that Swahili word. There are many forms of prostitution. To me, the worst is when the writer uses his God-given talent to prostitute a collective ideal. It is made even worse by his conviction that no prostitution is involved; it's all in the name of *bangsa* (race) and *semangat kebangsaan* (spirit of ethnic nationalism), you see. (We really must do something about that *kebangsaan* word; as long as we use it to mean nationalism or nationality, we'll continue to be trapped in the dark alley of atavism).

The Austrian satirist Karl Kraus (a Jew, of course) once ringingly announced his crusade as a writer by describing language as "a universal whore" which he must "turn into a virgin".

It's a big dream, a mammoth crusade, that one. But I believe every writer worth his/her salt must commit himself/herself to it. Otherwise, he/she might as well resign from the community of writers - and of human beings. In other words, commit literary *hara kiri*.

Testing the Parameter

[5th June 1991]

A veteran journalist and novelist who was at one time a top editor of this newspaper often used to challenge writers to "test the parameter".

'Parameter' in the sense here meant has been a vogue word for some time; freed from its precise meaning as a mathematical term, it is now vaguely synonymous with 'limit', 'boundary', 'standard', 'condition'. Mr Plain Words, Sir Ernest Gowers, who suspects showy users of the word of confusing it with 'perimeter', frowns upon this fashionable usage. He advises the wise writer to "watch it". I would advise our writers to "watch it" too. But not in Sir Ernest's sense; the 'it' I mean is something more important than the linguistic usage of 'parameter'. With our veteran journalist's challenge in mind, what our writers should watch are the needs of their creative spirit vis-a-vis the established 'parameter' or, if you like, 'perimeter'. That also means, in a sense, 'watching' the 'parameter'/'perimeter' itself. We all know that our censorship laws are very stringent. But, while hoping (and fighting?) for greater liberalism, it's not impossible to learn to live with them while we have to. You would be amazed what can be done within the existing restrictions. It's up to writers and publishers to exploit the limited freedom that exists. In other words to 'test the parameter' - or the perimeter of the permissible.

Self-censorship is a universal disease, but I believe its local manifestation is quite peculiar, very 'Malaysian' in an unflattering sense of the word. And what's more, it's becoming quite insidious. Those infected with this disease don't always realise it; even when they do, they try to pretend that it's unavoidable or justifiable. One can understand the self-censorship if the 'integrity' of the writer's *periok nasi* (rice bowl) is really at stake. But when it isn't and yet he still censors himself, one questions not so much his moral integrity as his intelligence. Basically, it's a question of perception - perception of what constitutes risks or dangers and the problem with our writers and literary middlemen (editors, publishers, judges

51

of literary competitions, members of literary award committees) is that too many of them tend to perceive dangers too readily. Ours is a highly 'sensitive' country, and people involved in the business of writing are extremely 'sensitive' people, not to things like stupidity, narrow-mindedness, corruption, threats to their freedom, but to the alleged sensitivity of certain subjects. Among these are, of course, race and religion. The law governing the expression of opinion on anything to do with these two subjects is admittedly forbidding because of its generality. But writers and editors should not allow this fact to breed needless fear in their minds. Yes, the particular opinion or perception might be unusual or unorthodox and likely to be absurdly misunderstood by fanatics or literal-minded ignoramuses. These people might even be stirred enough to make an issue of it in the Press. But this possibility, always present in our country, is not a legitimate ground for self-censorship. As long as the fuss is not likely to lead to a riot or cause dangerous bad feelings between the races or religious groups, controversies should always be welcomed, even if some of the participants in the controversies are fanatics or ignoramuses. Who knows, as a result of the controversy, the ignoramuses might even be enlightened. (The fanatics, of course, are not likely to change; but we can't allow them to rule our minds.)

There have been a few exceptions to this widespread fear in recent years; Kassim Ahmad's book on the *Hadith* is probably the most stiking. Kassim's book was eventually banned, but not until after it had generated a lively newspaper debate lasting a few months. The controversy didn't do anybody any harm; for the intellectual development of the country it, in fact, did some good. Ironically, the exceptions, instead of proving that it's possible to "test the parameter" or fun to try to push the perimeter of the permissible, seem to have had the opposite effect.

If self-censorship is bad for the general intellectual development of a country, it's worse for the development of its literature. I feel there is something about literature that makes self-censorship particularly bad for its health. Official censorship doesn't always have that effect, as the development of the literatures of Eastern European countries during the time of the Communist dictatorships testified. But as it involves creative writers, this self-censorship can be so ingrained in certain areas of thinking and feeling (that involving religion, say, or race) that it no longer appears like self-censorship. It operates at the level of the unconscious, even before the imagination can produce the germ of an idea or perception. Such writers can only be pitied, because without realising it, they have betrayed their calling. Perhaps the prevalence of such writers is one explanation for the general predictability of our literature today.

But let's imagine a novelist in our midst whose imagination is not captive to the insidious power of the group mind, who is free of the unconscious urge to censor that imagination. Let's imagine further that he has written a novel involving the subject of religion. It is unorthodox in some of its major perceptions, but not blasphemous or transgressive in the way *The Satanic Verses* is; in fact, it is full of reverence for the sacred, genuine reverence even if somewhat unusual. Now, what can he do if no publisher would publish it, and he is loath to censor himself because it would make the publication of his novel pointless? He can, of course, publish it himself, *samizdat*-style. But this requires money, and not many writers have it - especially writers who are cursed with the kind of mind that can think of such things in the first place.

One way out is for the novelist to resort to a literary device that would conceal his meaning to the vulgar majority or 'thought vigilantes'. This device can take the form of allegory, or something that involves the use of obscure symbolism and ambiguities. Some would claim that this strategy stinks of compromise; it is, in effect, self-censorship under another name. I don't think it is necessarily so. The problem with this kind of writing is not that it makes the writer's moral courage questionable, but it presupposes a sophisticated literary audience large enough to make the exercise worthwhile. If there is no such audience, as is the case in our country, the writing and publishing of such works become, frankly, not much more than literary masturbation. Allegorical and symbolical writings work in countries like Soviet Russia because there they have a sizable audience nurtured on the tradition of such writings and on serious literature generally.

So what can the Malaysian writer of this breed do? Nothing, really, other than commit literary suicide. Here in his homeland, or in 'a country elsewhere' - for exile for this kind of writer, who can only write about and for his people, would be tantamount to a literary suicide, too. He can, of course, keep on writing and hoarding up his manuscripts, hoping that one day the insidious disease of self-censorship among the middlemen of literature will cure itself. Unfortunately, this kind of disease doesn't easily cure itself; it's more likely to get worse. Actually, what is expected of our literary middlemen is nothing terribly heroic, just the simple exercise of their intelligence, or common sense - a quality needed to make them see that it's all right to take little risks in the area of imagination. In our situation, such little risks, which "test the parameter" or make minute little pushes at the perimeter of the permissible, can mean a great deal. It's a sad reflection of our state that even such an exercise of intelligence can require courage.

A young hero-worshipper in Bertolt Brecht's play *Galileo* says, "Unhappy is the land without a hero." His fallen hero, Galileo, a weak sensualist whose sensitivity to bodily pain had made him compromise, replies: "No. Unhappy is the land that needs a hero." I know what Galileo means, but I'd like to adapt that interesting line to our situation. I'd say: Unhappy is the land that needs a hero even for the things that don't really require a hero.

Rojak is Good for Nation Building

[1st July 1992]

The first of the nine challenges posed by Vision 2020 is that of creating by the second decade of the next century a united Malaysian nation which is ethnically integrated and harmonious. This amounts to an admission by the Government that, more than three decades after independence, we are still not a nation in the full sense of the word. Those of us who would agree with this belong to two main categories. There are the non-*Bumiputeras* who believe that the officially sanctioned 'Bumi/non-Bumi' dichotomy is the root of most of the obstacles to the emergence of a true nation. And there are the *Bumiputeras* who claim that we are not a true nation because we don't have linguistic and cultural unity. It is not my intention here to discuss all the reasons that have been offered for the absence of true nationhood. I only want to look at the linguistic reason advanced by the *Bumiputeras*, and to discuss it in relation to literature. Since literature is part of culture, what I have to say may have some bearing on the thorny issue of 'national culture'.

One of the many responses to our Prime Minister's call for a critical discussion of his Vision 2020 is a booklet I've just read called *Wawasan 2020 dan Pembinaan Bangsa Malaysia* (Vision 2020 and the Building of a Malaysian Nation). Published by the Department of Anthropology and Sociology, Universiti Kebangsaan Malaysia (National University of Malaysia), the booklet is the result of a dialogue held last year by a group of UKM academics. The views expressed in it can be considered representative of the dominant thinking among the Malay intellectual elite.

All the academics in the dialogue more or less agree that the two main reasons for the failure of a true Malaysian nation to emerge are: 1) the unwillingness of the majority of non-Bumis and a section of the Bumi elite to show a genuine and full commitment to the national language; 2) the persistence of cultural pluralism despite demands by the Bumi literati for a full implementation of the National Cultural Policy. The academics are particularly concerned about the continuing presence of the language of our former colonial masters. They lament the fact that English is still very visible everywhere in this country; on TV, in the print media, in all forms of advertising, on shop signs, at the cinemas, in bookshops and other places. In the private sector, English is the dominant language of communication. Private colleges with English as the medium of instruction are allowed to function freely. These academics further complain that even the younger generation of non-*Bumis* who were educated in the National Language prefer to speak English or their own language when there is no official compulsion or expectation for them to speak in the National Language. With TV watching constituting a large portion of their leisure time and English newspapers, magazines and books their preferred reading material, it is not surprising that English is their usual medium of communication. But what the UKM academics are really sad about is the fact that a sizable section of the Malay elite, especially the businessmen, prefer to speak in English not only to non-*Bumis* but among themselves too. What's worse, they even think in English!

The Government is taken to task for compromising on the issue of national language; for allowing English to be so visible in many areas of public life. The Government, it is repeatedly stressed in the dialogue, must apply the law rigorously to ensure that only the National Language is used in situations where such use is legally enforceable. It is even implied that the Government should extend its legal powers, presumably through new acts of Parliament or amendments to the present National Language Act, to ensure that the status of Malay as the sole official language is respected. The implication is strengthened by the proposal that there should be a National Culture Act to correspond with the National Language Act. Such an act, it is argued, would ensure the end of *kebudayaan rojak* (salad culture) - a colloquial expression for 'cultural pluralism' or 'multi-culturalism'.

One of the academics is sceptical about the fifth challenge posed by Vision 2020, that of creating a liberal and tolerant society in which Malaysians respect each other's creeds and customs. He wonders if this is not an approval of *kebudayaan rojak*. Another even more uncompromising academic actually accuses the Prime Minister of inserting the dangerous idea of "democratisation of culture" in his Vision 2020. This same academic categorically asserts that *"nasionalisme Malaysia bereti ... nasionalisme bumiputera, dan Wawasan 2020 perlu didukung oleh nasionalisme bumiputera ini"* ("Malaysian nationalism means ... *Bumiputera* nationalism, and Vision 2020 must be buttressed by this *Bumiputera* nationalism"). He also prophesies that if the present widespread use of English is not checked, *"bangsa Malaysia pada tahun 2020 ialah bangsa yang fasih dalam bahasa Inggeris."* ("the Malaysian nation in the year 2020 will be a nation fluent in the English language") (I didn't know that to be fluent in the *lingua franca* of the world is a bad thing.)

The booklet as a whole strikes me as a rather regressive document which shows that ethnocentric thinking is still very strong among the *Bumi* intellectual elite. They are not yet psychologically liberated, to use a phrase from Vision 2020. The document weakens even more the little faith that sceptics like me have in our ability to meet the challenges of creating a united nation which is ethnically integrated, and a mature democratic society which is psychologically liberated, liberal and tolerant. The suggestion in the booklet that non-*Bumis* who don't speak the National Language all or most of the time are *ipso facto* not Malaysian in spirit, and those *Bumis* who are bilingual are renegrades, is nonsense. And the allegation that the non-*Bumis* are more conscious of their ethnic identities than their identity as Malaysians is only worth entertaining if the UKM academics are prepared to be honest about the *Bumis'* own sense of identity. Aren't they also like the non-*Bumis* in this respect? One of the academics actually admits it, and I commend him for his honesty.

On the question of cultural pluralism, we must be realistic. As realists have often pointed out, *kebudayaan rojak* is inevitable given the multi-ethnic nature of our society in which no one race truly dominates in terms of numbers. Anyway, what's wrong with *kebudayaan rojak*? Malaysians like *rojak*. It's good for them, and it helps nation-building. Unity in diversity is certainly better for the vitality of our cultural life than the imposition of an artificially conceived national culture through legislation. A living culture, as everyone knows, grows naturally; it cannot be programmed or legislated according to an abstract recipe. And it is disingenuous of the UKM academics to blame linguistic diversity, in particular, for the failure of a true Malaysian nation to emerge. There are other factors, mainly political, which are really responsible.

As far as English is concerned, its widespread use can, under the right conditions, be good for the nation because, like Bahasa Malaysia, English cuts across ethnic differences. Why regret the fact that our country has more that one *lingua franca*? Isn't it better for unity and integration? I'd even be reckless enough to argue that in the present state of affairs, English is perhaps a better medium of integration, certainly among middle and lower middle class Malaysians, than even the National Language. Why? Because it is not identified with any particular ethnic group. And if we confine ourselves to the middle and lower middle classes, more non chauvinists are found among English-speaking Malaysians than among speakers of the other languages.

This is something that could make our English language novelists, poets, dramatists and essayists more sensitive to the dream of true nationhood and more alert to the evils of chauvinism. The ability of the National Language to bring about national integration is not in question here. But national integration is a very slow process; we could do with any help we can get in making it less slow. The English language, I think, can be a help here. And it doesn't really matter that English is largely the language of the elite and its potential as a medium of integration is mainly confined to the middle class. This is after all the class from which most of our leaders come. And in the slow process of true nation-building, our leaders must show the way instead of being led by the masses in the name of political expediency.

Neither A Campaign Nor A Conspiracy

[19th February 1992]

The president of Gapena (National Federation of Writers' Associations) has finally spoken in response to "The Big Q" that I raised in this column. "The Big Q", you'll remember, had to do with that mysterious something called 'National Literature', and some other issues closely related to it. The Gapena President, Datuk Prof Ismail Hussein, chose to speak up on the question at a book launch rather than on this page, as many people would have expected, since the question was raised here. One can only guess at his reasons. No doubt his professed aversion to writing to an English-language newspaper, especially on issues such as this, was one of them. It is also possible that he knew a public speech would get him a wide media coverage. All the major papers reported his speech, and typically they sensationalised even more what was already quite sensational in the Datuk's speech. With one surprising exception, all the reports played up the Datuk's claim that the columnist who raised "The Big Q" (the Datuk preferred not to mention my name) was guilty, at least by implication, of questioning the status of Malay as the National Language and therefore (God help me!) the constitution.

I was there when the Datuk gave his speech, That speech, let me say it straight, grossly distorted and perverted the views I expressed in this column. I never, even by implication however remote or devious, ever suggested what was claimed by the Datuk. In fact I took great care to stress in one column that "No one with even a nodding acquaintance with history would question the status of Malay as our National Language." The Datuk would, of course, say that by raising certain questions concerning the idea of National Literature, I was *ipso facto* guilty of questioning the constitutional status of the National Language. I personally cannot see the logic of this. The constitution has nothing to say about 'National Literature', just as it has nothing to say about 'National Art', 'National Music', 'National Architecture', 'National Food' or National Whatever. And what I did in this column was simply to raise certain questions with the idea of initiating an intelligent critical discussion on the concept of a National Literature and other related issues. To initiate a simple discussion or debate - that was all. I had the faint hope that such a debate might for once lead to something approximating a real dialogue among Malaysians. I thought I could be of some service here because I write in both languages. And I do keep in touch with what's happening in Malay writing and even have a few like-minded friends whom I respect among the *sasterawans* (writers). Yes, a debate, and perhaps a dialogue. That was the intention of my discourse. I wasn't part of any "campaign", a loaded word the Datuk used repeatedly in his highly tendentious speech. And it certainly wasn't part of any conspiracy with the innocent Salleh Ben Joned being used as a tool (by some invisible Anti-*Bumi* League, remote-controlled by some Zionist organisation perhaps?), as is believed in certain quarters. 'Conspiracy' is often the first thing that comes to the minds of people who are intellectually bankrupt. Perhaps my manner was a bit too provocative, which my fellow *Bumis* cannot take. I am sorry about that, but really I couldn't help it. I am a big mouth who gets bored quite easily, and can be disastrously impatient and dismissively ironic with certain types - the solemnly pompous; the parochial, witless (in both senses of 'wit') *katak-bawah-tempurung* (frogs under a coconut shell) types, full of phoney *seni* (art) but cannot see beyond their automatic pieties; the *cendekiawans* (intellectuals) trapped in their borrowed abstractions and puritanical patriotic clichés, the ... That's enough, Salleh Ben! Don't make yourself more obnoxious than you have already. Your tone is dangerously 'un-Malay'. See what the Gapena President has made of it. Yes, the Datuk accused me of denigrating Malay literature and writers. It seems he couldn't make the distinction between being ironically dismissive of certain types of *sasterawans* and denigrating Malay literature and Malay writers as a whole. The word 'types' suggests exceptions, Datuk; and please note that on a number of occassions, I have paid tribute to those striking exceptions among our *sasterawans*, exceptions which must grow in number if our literary *kaum* (community) is not to be the laughing stock of the big world.

People read into anything what they want. In my case, the tone I tend to adopt has apparently been the undoing of me as a trusted member of my race. There is, it seems, a certain image of Salleh Ben Joned among our *sasterawans*, and their reading of whatever I write is conditioned by that image. There is not much I can do about it; even if I were to say tomorrow that I love our *sasterawans* and mean it, they won't believe me. Sometimes I wonder whether the whole thing is worth it. I can go on about the subject, but after a while, when the relevant people are not getting the point of what you are saying, it gets boring even for the biggest of big-mouths. Maybe the 'devil's disciple' in me (if there is such a presence) loves indulging in communal masochism for the ringside entertainment of non-*Bumis*. It has, in fact, been suggested that I am a preverse *Bumi*, my *sasterawan*-bashing trips nothing but a shameless act of pandering to the English educated with their alleged anti-Bumi prejudices. I think my fellow *Bumis* should seriously examine themselves. Ask themselves: for how long must we be defensive, insecure, afraid to criticise ourselves in full view of our non-*Bumi* fellow Malaysians? For how long must any open criticism of the kind made in *AIP* be considered *ipso facto* a denigration, a racial slur or insult? Must we so easily continue to feel *hina* (a word with powerful connotations, much stronger than the English 'insult')? (Another established sentimental *sasterawan* has been going around saying that I *"menghina sastera dan sasterawan Melayu"* "Hold in contempt Malay writers and Malay literature.) I think there is some kind of communal neurosis here that might need the help of a good *bomoh* (medicine man) for a cure. I stubbornly persist (for how much longer, I can't say though) in believing that there is yet some hope that our writings will give real meaning to the idea of being 'Malaysian'. Though in my discourse on "The Big Q", I merely raised certain questions without actually formulating my own stand on the subject of National Literature/Malaysian literature, there were enough hints, I thought, as to what my own stand was. I personally think it is enough to have a National Language without having to have a National Literature as well. The very idea of a National Literature is dubious and serves no civilised purpose, certainly not that of true 'nation building'. As far as I know, this is the only country in the world that feels it needs one, and the need suggests a feeling of insecurity. Frankly, in our case, a National Literature, tightly conceived and jealously guarded as it is, is mainly good for providing protection to second and third rate writers against the competition of writers who write in languages that disqualify them from being part of the select band. To insist on a 'National Literature' is to betray a fundamental lack of understanding of what literature is all about. Just as to insist on a 'National Art', 'National Music', 'National Food' is to show a total misconception of what art, music and food are all about. "All true art is national," said a distinguished art critic, "but National Art is bad."

The Gapena President in his speech has finally conceded (apparently) that writings in languages other than Malay could be considered "Malaysian literature" (he used to call them "sectional", "communal", "immigrant" and whatnot). But predictably, he still vigorously insisted that they could not, and could never be part of the holy 'National Literature'. All right. I'd say let him and the Gapena *kaum* keep their 'National Literature' and do what they like with it. True writers don't care for categories and labels, anyway. It's the spirit and the art that matter. And if our Malaysian writer is a true writer, sensitive to the realities (social, political, moral, religious, mythical, metaphysical) of his/her environment, who could experience the joys and the pains, the dreams and the terrors of our people, could hear as well the redeeming and transforming 'other voice' of his art, then he/she is the writer we all need, who can make us proud of being Malaysian and at the same time part of the civilised community of mankind. The Gapena President had a lot to say about the Vision 2020 in that speech of his. In my view, that vision of a truly advanced united Malaysian nation could only become a reality if people in the position of moulding opinions, values and dreams drop their hang-ups, regressive sentiments and stereotype thinking. And this is where our writers writing 'Malaysian literature', with or without that precious label of 'National', can play a major part.

Once Again, English, *Our* English

[5th January 1994]

All the Malay and English newspapers, except one, gave it banner headlines. And so they should. It was one of the most important speeches the Prime Minister gave in 1993. It announced a significant shift in the Government's policy on the use of English as a medium of instruction in the universities. Once again Dr Mahathir showed quiet determination not to allow sentimental pieties over language to be a dead weight that slows down the country's march towards the dream year 2020. The commitment to the total use of Bahasa Malaysia (Malay Language) in every area of learning, especially in science and technology, has turned out to be problematic. Shortage of qualified teachers capable of teaching in BM, of competent translators who could make available essential texts existing only in English - these are among the major factors that have made a slight change in strategy necessary, without, however, compromising fundamental commitments and principles or the sense of national pride. Permitting the use of (or a return to) English as the medium of instruction in such technical subjects as medicine, engineering and computer science is the logical thing to do under the circumstances. The language is already there, part of our colonial inheritance; what is needed now is to make that particular inheritance whole and healthy again, and to undo the damage done to it (a serious decline in standards mainly) by fanatical nationalistic enthusiasms over the decades since Independence. And to do this without feeling any guilt, of being assailed by the sense of having betrayed our sacred identity as Malaysians (for the chauvinists, 'identity as Malays', no doubt). The slogan *Bahasa Jiwa Bangsa* (language is the soul of the nation) does have a degree of truth in it, so long as we are not too literal or rigid about both 'language' and 'soul'.

The Government's decision may be entirely pragmatic in its motivation. The concern behind it is the pursuit of progress. In particular, the target of a fully developed, highly competitive nation respected by the world in the year 2020. It has become a compulsive ritual now that every time a good word is said about English, immediate assurance about the sacred status of the National Language is given. No one wants to be misunderstood, least of all a politician, and on such a sacrosanct matter too. It has happened before (remember last year, when the Prime Minister's very faith in BM was questioned?) - and there's no guarantee it won't happen again. So the Prime Minister again gave his assurance in that speech of his. And two days later, to make assurance doubly sure, his new Deputy also gave his. "In 1993," he said, "we are more confident of the strength of Bahasa Malaysia" (note, he said 'Malaysia' not 'Melayu') ... There should be no cause for concern if we want our younger generation to improve their English." Anwar even reminded Malaysians that the Nineties are not like the Sixties - that decade of tension when he was a troublesome student leader in Universiti Malaya. (Remember?). Outside the area with which the Prime Minister's speech was immediately concerned, the place of Bahasa Malaysia as the first language of the nation is secure - even if only in the public sector, not the private. This officially-sanctioned return of English for a specific practical purpose is not only *not* a threat to the status of Bahasa Malaysia; it will also, said the Prime Minister, benefit the National Language itself in the long run.

The idea that giving English its proper and necessary place in our life can even help BM is something new in Dr M's thinking and public utterance on the question of language. "We are of the opinion," he said, "that once we emerge as a successful race (nation?), our language will also be successful and will gain respect." This opinion was echoed by a number of academic and public figures, the Deputy Vice-Chancellor of Universiti Pertanian Malaysia (Malaysian Agricultural University) being one of them. So 'success' is the keyword - key to everything, including the attainment of that position which compels the respect of the entire world. The reactions from the academics and intellectuals to Dr M's speech have been generally favourable. A few voiced anxiety that the move would be at the expense of Bahasa Malaysia. A group of Universiti Kebangsaan Malaysia lecturers wrote a very pertinent letter to the *New Straits Times* (Jan 1) saying that, while they are not opposed to the necessary shift in policy, it's not enough for the Government to do just that. The whole education system, they rightly say, needs to be reformed, particularly as it applies to the teaching of English. Language is the Soul of the Nation. Successful Malaysia in the 2020's will have her 'soul' expressed in BM, helped not a little by a judiciously pragmatic use of the world's *lingua franca* and most convenient means to economic and technological competitiveness. But what kind of 'soul'? And will this Malaysian soul be expressed only in BM, leaving English as the means of expressing non-spiritual or purely secular material needs? If you asked the president of Gapena he would probably say, absolutely, yes - i.e. if he could forgive the Mahathir government even that minimum role granted to English.

I have argued in this column more than once that English was playing and would continue to play an important role not only in our relations with the rest of the world, but within our own multi-ethnic society. And that role is by no means merely economic, scientific or technological. After more than three decades of independence, and despite the National Education Policy, English is still used widely in our country. And what's important, that use cuts across ethnic boundaries. Now, with the slogan or motto *Bahasa Jiwa Bangsa* in mind, would any unblinkered Malaysian say that our 'Malaysian soul', however ill-defined and ambiguous it may be, can only be expressed in the National Language? A language belongs to those who speak it. It's as simple as that. Given this fact, and that language communicates experience and is capable of transcending the boundaries of the culture of its origin - given all this, then the English we speak in Malaysia today belongs to us. It's *our* English; along with BM it expresses our 'soul', with all its contradictions and confusions, as much as our social and material needs.

The idea that true nationhood is impossible without a native language to express that sense is not always true. Just look at Ireland. Much of the spirit of her rebellion against England was expressed in the English language. Ireland in fact made the language of her colonial masters her own, and defined herself in that language. In the process, she produced some of the greatest writers in English. Though Ireland and Malaysia do have certain things in common (most of them not very nice), the two countries are very different otherwise. For one, unlike the virtually dead

Gaelic (the native language of that republic), BM is very much alive. Unlike poor Ireland, therefore, we Malaysians have more than one language in which to express our 'soul'. Isn't that all the better?

Be Sophisticated and Silly All the Way

[12th January 1994]

It was a use of words that an alert observer would call ambiguous, if not confusing. A political scientist would probably call it *skilfully* ambiguous. Thus the Deputy Prime Minister's statement on the language issue after a meeting with members of the Kongres Cendekiawan Melayu (KCM), or Congress of Malay Intellectuals, last Friday. "I have explained (to the KCM delegation)," said Anwar, "that while existing policy with regard to the use of the National Language will be continued, there will be *greater emphasis* on English." (My italics.) Some people wouldn't consider 'greater emphasis' the same as allowing the use of English as the medium of instruction in the limited area specified. Emphasis would merely suggest that the generally accepted status of English as an important second language would be given a fuller practical meaning, and that more strenuous efforts be made and more effective methods used to ensure that our students acquire a better command of the language. I wouldn't have thought that Anwar's words of assurance would satisfy those Malay nationalists who had earlier opposed the limited return of English as announced by the Prime Minister on Dec 27 and reconfirmed after last Saturday's meeting of the Umno Supreme Council. I don't know whether those words of Anwar as quoted in the *New Straits Times* (Jan 8) reflect what he actually said to the Malay intellectuals at the two-hour closed-door meeting. In any case it's good news that the delegation of anxious intellectuals, including the President of Gapena, were "satisfied with Anwar's assurance that there would not be any change to the Government's policy". Which must mean they've dropped their earlier opposition to the Government's move. Move is, I think, more accurate here than 'change of policy', however slight or peripheral that alleged change may be. The decision to allow a return to English for the limited area specified was probably meant to be taken (though Dr Mahathir didn't say so) as a stop-gap measure - that is, English would be used until there are enough lecturers *fully qualified* to teach science and technology in Bahasa Malaysia (Malay Language), and enough text and reference books on those technical subjects have been *competently* translated into Bahasa Malaysia. I hope the reported acceptance by the KCM of the Government's assurance will be followed by similar acceptance by other groups, academic and intellectual. But it is just a hope, probably without much basis.

The curious case of the KCM aside, I've been led to believe that, in my column last Wednesday, I'd underestimated the resistance to the Government's move. This was after learning that my passing reference to the group of UKM (Universiti Kebangsaan Malaysia) lecturers who wrote a letter to *NST* was not quite accurate; one of the signatories to the letter told me I was wrong in saying that those lecturers were 'not opposed' to the apparent 'policy shift'. (He did acknowledge, however, that I can't really be blamed for the error; due to editorial cuts, the letter was not crystal clear on the issue and could easily be read the way I read it.) It seems that there are not a few academics and intellectuals who either remain suspicious of the Government's intention or are simply opposed to the return to English, temporary or otherwise, for the teaching of science and technology. Take the *Utusan Malaysia* columnist and ISIS Fellow, Rustam A. Sani. This highly vocal scholar feared that, what was described by the *NST* writer who interviewed him as a "peripheral adjustment in the language policy", was perhaps "the beginning of more". And he sadly wondered if it didn't signify that "the cultural programme that came with the National Language policy has failed", and that "the Malay language cannot cope with progress". (*NST*, Jan 2) In his *Utusan* column of Jan 3, Rustam elaborated on this question of double 'failure'. It's an interesting piece and quite passionately argued. And I must admit that, though I'd taken this son of a noted nationalist to task for the unfair attitude to our English-language writers he expressed, I found his article last week strangely quite moving. Yes, I did say 'moving'. You see, I am not 'anti-Malay' as some *sasterawans* think. (How can I be when I write in both Malay and English?) It's just that I'm not ideologically rigid about language and national identity, and very much an incorrigible pluralist in cultural matters. I consider it a privilege, not an ideological shortcoming, for our nation to be bilingual. Other countries not so well-blessed and not sentimental about their native languages must envy us.

I don't suppose it's any good to tell Rustam Sani that the Government's "peripheral adjustment" to the language policy is not necessarily "the beginning of something more". But I'd still like to share with him my modest thoughts about some of the reasons for the apparent 'failure' of the project of modernising BM, of transforming it into a language fit for a nation striving to be fully developed and industrialised by the year 2020. (I won't say anything about the other 'failure', that of the "cultural programme that came with the National Language policy". This is because the "cultural programme" Rustam referred to is not something that I as a pluralist would endorse.) First, let me say it loud and clear that I agree with Rustam that the apparent 'failure' of the project of modernising our country through the Malay language is not due to any inherent fault of that language. Having agreed with Rustam on this general point, I must now say where and how 'we' have failed. Since the 'we' here includes bilinguists like me, I'd of course dismiss any contention that one of the reasons for the 'failure' is the continued widespread use of English. I believe we can be bilingual and at the same time committed to the modernisation of BM. Now, why has the modernisation of BM for the purpose of making it a fit medium of instruction in science and technology failed? For reason of space, I'll only deal with this failure as it is manifested in the vital project of translation and, to a much lesser extent, as it is manifested in the current fate of the Malay language in the hands of Malay academics and writers themselves. I'll say it bluntly: the translation project has largely failed because incompetent people, without proper training, qualification and experience, have been chosen to do most of the translations. This has been made worse by sheer bureaucratic short-sightedness and incompetence that have made the realisation of the vital project incredibly slow - so slow that three-and-a-half decades after independence our university libraries can only boast a very, very tiny percentage of text and reference books in BM. And of that tiny percentage, not a few are hopeless, either inaccurate or simply unreadable, because they are so badly translated. The responsiblity for this lies mainly with Dewan Bahasa dan Pustaka, since it is the body entrusted with the translation project. I'd describe the approach to this project - that is, the attitude behind it - as *cincai* (a Malay word of Chinese origin, meaning, 'casual, done in a shoddy manner and readily accepted, however shoddy'). This attitude, as we all know, is typically Malaysian, if not Malay.

Now, this *cincai* attitude goes very well with another tendency of our academics, intellectuals and *sasterawans*. And that is the tendency to corrupt that very language whose honour they are so noisily concerned with. They are so easily seduced and befuddled by the sound of new words and jargon of English origin or old Malay words refurbished for flashy rhetorical purposes, that they end up by making Malay so ugly or unreadable or both (see my piece *The Transformasi of a Language*, AIP, June 12, 1991). When these academic corrupters of the Malay language or their pupils do translation, God help us! If the original English is barely readable (as in books or academic articles on the latest Western literary or sociological theory, or philosophy of science), they make the translation worse than unreadable. To use a refurbished old Malay word, they are so desparate in wanting to sound *canggih* (sophisticated) that they sound awful and don't make much sense. Ironically enough, the word *canggih*, which is so popular now (Rustam has "*moden dan canggih*" (sophisticated and modern) in that column of his), used to mean the opposite of what it means now. *Kamus Dewan* (1984 edition), terribly out of date obviously, has only one entry. What is it? Believe it or not, that single entry says *canggih* means *terlalu banyak bercakap* (talks too much, or in one word, 'bullshits'). That's a characteristic of intellectuals and politicians, isn't it? Someone who knows Javanese told me that in that language it means or used to mean 'gaudy' (like having too much cheap make-up). In Wilkinson's Malay-English Dictionary (1903), there's no *canggih*; but there's *chenggeh*, which must be a northern dialect variation of *canggih*. The meaning? 'Affected, dandified'. Now, isn't that very interesting? So, scribblers and bullshitters of Malaysia, unite! In one homogenous voice, be *canggih* and *cincai* all the way to the year 2020. You have nothing to lose but your brains.

The *Transformasi* of a Language

[12th June 1991]

In Alexander Solzhenitsyn's novel *The First Circle*, there is an odd character, Dimitry Sologdin, an engineer in a 'special prison' built by Stalin for highly qualified political prisoners. Sologdin is obsessed with the purity of his beloved native language. He is disgusted with the habit of many Russian writers of polluting the Russian language with the indiscriminate fashionable borrowings from the West. The disgust is so strong that when he catches himself inadvertently committing the offence, he makes a tick on a sheet of paper ... The ticks are penalty marks, and he punishes himself according to how many there are. I don't fancy Sologdin's masochism, but I do share his disgust with the habit of borrowing foreign words when there is no need for it.

All languages borrow from others, but the borrowing should be dictated by necessity, not fashion, laziness, pretentiousness, or any other self-indulgent motive. Bahasa Malaysia writers in general are prone to this habit of indiscriminate borrowing from English. This is not a recent phenomenon; it has been with us ever since *Merdeka* (Independence). The ironical thing is that the worst culprits are not the English-educated whose Malay vocabulary is poor and who are too lazy or too uninterested to do anything about it. No, the worst culprits are the Malay-educated, especially those who make a lot of noise about the sanctity of the National Language. These writers, especially the literary critics, borrow, in some cases kidnap, English words not because they are desperately poor in BM vocabulary, but because they are desperately in need of ego-boosting, or something with which to dress up the poverty of their ideas. When you have nothing to say, big foreign words, the more abstract the better, can be quite handy. I think it is the Indonesians who taught them, or encouraged them in this pernicious habit. Indonesian writers have always been thoroughly indiscriminate in their borrowing of European words. (That lively Indonesian weekly *Tempo* is for me quite painful to read, despite its solid critical content.) Malay writers who have always looked up to their cousins across the Straits cannot resist copying them. They have always felt inferior when dealing with them; witness the way they ape the Indonesian accent when reading poetry or when speaking to Indonesian writers. Even those who should know better can't resist the temptation to pollute the language. One distinguished novelist, I remember, thought that the simple Malay word *petikan* (quotation) was not distinguished enough; so he coined a new word, *kotasi*. It was this same novelist who came up with the inspired BM term for playwright, *peliriat*. This one never became popular, presumably because of its unintentionally obscene sound. The whole business is really quite *absud* (pronounced "absood"), to borrow a wonderful *transformasi* (transformation) of 'absurd' by a theatre enthusiast.

It is revealing that the most commonly borrowed English word in Malay *puisi* (poetry) is also a ghastly mistake. The word is *antologi* which has become a standard word now. Malay poets use the word to mean collection or selection of poems by an individual poet. 'Anthology' in English means a collection of poems or writings by various writers. There is a good Malay word for a collection or selection (*kumpulan, pilihan*), and when a Malay word for a real anthology is required there is that wonderful word *Bunga Rampai* or *Rampaian. Bunga Rampai* is literally a posy, which is interesting because the word 'anthology' itself is from the Greek *anthologia* meaning a flower-gathering.

The worst polluters of the Malay language are, of course, the critics or *kritikus* (this one I like; it's unintentionally apt - apt because *tikus* in Malay means rat). I remember one hyperactive *kritikus* in an article on drama trying to numb his readers with obscenities like *mistikus, audienisma, mentransformasikan, pengkonsenterasian* (he must have nearly choked on that one). And this is how one academic *kritikus* writes about the poetry of one of our most sensitive poets:

" ... *dalam hubungan konteks pada proses exteriorization dan interiorization lahir perilaku-perilaku osilasi dan stasis organisme...* " ("... in the context of the process of exteriorization and interiorization, emerges features of oscillation and organic stasis ...")

72

Talk of critics mauling and pulverising poetry! If much of what goes under the name of literary criticism in English today is quite unreadable, in Malay it's even worse. Malay literary critics love theories and the horrible jargon spawned by them; when it comes to Western literature most of them seem to read nothing but theories and criticism, not the creative works themselves. I have often been struck by the ease with which they co-opt the latest structuralist or post-structuralist jargon (not always accurately), and by their ignorance of specific Western poems, plays or novels.

I won't be surprised if in the year 2020, we get a 'writerly' (post-structuralist jargon, this) *kritikus* from one of our univerities, with perhaps a PhD from the University of Buffalo, writing like this:

> *"Situasi sastera kontemporari Malaysia memanifestasikan sindrom-sindrom dan episteme kekrisisian; sindrom yang dominan ialah sindrom alienasi yang bermulti-level, bermulti-dimensi dan berkontradiksi antara sinkronisasi dan diakronisasi - alienasi sosial, alienasi kultural, alienasi komunal, alienasi intelectuil, alienasi metafisikal, alienasi literisasi; totalitinya adalah konsekuensi kontradiksi dan tensyen antara tradisi dan modenisasi, osilasi stasis antara pretensi dan mediokriti, authentisma dan autistisma ..."* ("The situation of contemporary Malaysian literature manifests the syndromes and epistemes of crisis; the dominant syndromes being those of alienation which are multi-level, multi-dimensional and full of contradictions between synchronism and diachronism - social alienation, cultural alienation, intellectual alienation, literalistic alienation; the totality of which is the consequence of contradictions and tensions between tradition and modernization, static oscillation between pretension and mediocrity, authenticity and autistism ...")

What a wonderful way of *bermastibasi* (masturbation) and *berbulshitasi* (bullshit)! You'd need a PhD from Universiti *Kerbau* (buffalo) to be able to do that.

Anti-Islam and all that Jazz

[26th June 1991]

There is a type of thinking about literature in Malay critical writing today that I find deeply disturbing. It is a type of thinking that would make our literature a closed system, all in the name of 'the true or pure Malay-Islamic tradition'. 'True Malay', mind you. There's no concern with the truly Malaysian, despite all the fuss about the National Language and the ideals it's supposed to embody. As is usual with such thinking, it tends to resort to highly-charged emotive language when arguing against its opponents. Condemnatory labelling of opponents designed to put them beyond the pale of the Malay-Islamic world is not infrequent. 'Anti-Malay' and 'anti-Islamic' are the ultimate weapons of condemnation. And we all know what it means in this country to be called 'anti-Malay' or 'anti-Islam'. It's like being labelled 'pro-Communist' or 'un-American' during the witch-hunting 'McCarthy Era' in the USA.

This is a crude strategy one would expect of the hack journalist, fundamentalist demagogue or chauvinistic politician who writes for the mob, but not of the critic with a pretension to scholarship. Such a critic is one Mohd Affandi Hassan who is currently engaged in an offensive on behalf of what he considers 'pure Malay' (read 'Islamic') concept of literature in the widely circulated literary monthly *Dewan Sastera*. His target is Professor Muhammad Haji Salleh of Universiti Kebangsaan Malaysia (National University of Malaysia). It was Professor Muhammad's inaugural lecture, called *Puitika Melayu* (Malay Poetics), delivered at UKM two years ago and subsequently published, which provoked Encik Affandi into writing a lengthy still ongoing polemic full of pompous fashionable talk about 'domains' and 'systems' in literature. Professor Muhammad uses some current Western literary theories to formulate or speculate about the conceptual basis of traditional Malay literature. Encik Affandi thinks that the professor's allegedly misguided use of such theories has made him guilty of worshipping the West ("*pemujaan kepada Barat*"). As if that wasn't bad enough, he further accuses the poor professor of "*berlebihan memuja tinggalan animisme dan Hindu-Buddha*" ("excessively worshipping the survivals of animism and Hindu-Buddhism"), and therefore of having an attitude that is "*sangat anti-Islam*" ("very anti-Islamic"), simply because the professor has some positive things to say about the unstated theory behind certain pre-Islamic Malay literary/ cultural forms. Professor Muhammad rightly considered the label 'anti-Islam', repeated several times in the first part of Encik Affandi's polemic, as defamatory, and took legal action. But the case didn't make it to the courts; Malay civility finally triumphed with the publication of an apology by Encik Affandi and Dewan Bahasa in the current issue of *Dewan Sastera*. I hope this incident will be a lesson to other fanatical and shrill defenders of the purity of Malay-Islamic values.

In this modest column, I don't wish to enter the debate between these two *gergasi* (giants) of Malay literary theory. I am not a scholar of Malay literature, and I am hopelessly 'Westernised'. The views I have about traditional Malay literature are those of an idiosyncratic layman, and they are probably outrageous enough to provoke people like Encik Affandi into calling me all kinds of things. And that can be dangerous. What I would like to do here is make a few comments on certain things Encik Affandi says which I think I know something about. Encik Affandi believes with his guru, Professor Syed Naquib al-Attas, that Islam radically and totally transformed the Malay world-view, sensibility and concept of literature. Because of that, it is considered dangerously atavistic to talk of the survival and influence of pre-Islamic literary concepts and values. The claim of total transformation from pre-Islamic to Islamic concept of aesthetic values is, I think, highly arguable, but it is not what I want to argue here. What I would like to take up is Encik Affandi's claim that after a long period of Islamic concep-tual dominance, embodied in literary forms of Islamic origins like the *hikayat* and *syair*, the Malay concept of literature underwent another radical, but this time corrupting transformation under the influence of Westernisation. Like many others who think like him, he indiscriminately lumps all Western literary influence as 'totally secularistic', in the sense of being hostile to things spiritual or metaphysical. This is like the popular tendency to identify every-thing Western with materialism (in both the philosophical and moral sense, though the latter is usually meant). Although it is true that secularism and philosophical materialism did come with Westernisation, it is a gross distortion of Western literary ideas and practice to say that the influence of Western concepts of literature, as embodied in Western-inspired forms like the novel, *puisi* (poetry) and drama, has meant 'total secularism'. No one with even a superficial first-hand acquaintance with Western literature would make such a claim. There are Western writers who are thoroughly secular (especially those influenced by Marxism), but many of them, including some of the great modernists, even the apostates among them, were consumed by a hunger for the transcendent, had an acute sense of the sacred however unorthodox or anti-doctrinal, and were certainly fiercely critical of the spiritually impoverished nature of modern man's existence. Only a person with a deficient notion of spirituality would say that a rejection of established doctrinal religions necessarily means the rejection of spirituality and the embracing of 'materialism'.

A preoccupation with man's spiritual needs has certainly always been a continuing and essential part of Western poetry. Even the novel, the dominant, supposedly secular, literary form is not necessarily anti-spiritual. The focus of the novel may be social man, but it doesn't preclude the exploration of spiritual and metaphysical themes. Far from it. Encik Affandi's ignorant dismissal of all modern literature ("*sastera moden seluruhnya*"), including modern Malaysian literature formally influenced by it, as reflecting "the writer's spiritual emptiness" ("*kekosongan jiwa penulis*") is so incredible that it is not worth arguing against. It's clear to me that Encik Affandi, the zealous champion of what he takes to be the true Malay concept of literature, has an incredibly rigid and closed notion of the spiritual in literature. And he clearly uses the word 'secular' to mean anything he considers 'un-Islamic', and therefore 'un-Malay'. His weird concept of literature and writing in general is so closed that he even (not surprisingly, I'd say) questions the involvement of non-Malays ("*kaum imigran*" "immigrant community") in Bahasa Malaysia writing. Their motives, he says, are highly dubious and the consequence of their involvement, together with that of the "total secularisation" of literature, is a "new barbarism" ("*kebiadaban baru*")! 'Barbarism' indeed! I wonder which truly comes under that category - the target of his attack or the kind of thinking behind that attack.

Muslim Writers and the Apostasy Law

[3rd November 1993]

Sacrilege, blasphemy, polytheism, and apostasy are the four terrors of the Muslim mind. Not unlike having four nasty wives. I've been haunted by them, grappled with them, screamed at them, cursed them, damned them. Of the four, I'm not sure which one is the nastiest or the most dangerous. But as a writer, I'm somewhat more intrigued by the fourth than the others, or, to sustain the marital analogy for a moment longer, the youngest, the prettiest and most ambiguously seductive one. For a long time, on and off (more off than on, for reason's which should in a minute be obvious), I've been consulting the Quran, hoping for some way of resolving my ambivalent nocturnal relations with this temptress, whose Arabic name (*riddah*) is inscrutably ironic: it's not that easy to get rid of her once she has slipped into your semi-conscious self, with all the ardour of her ambiguity.

I've been thinking and thinking about one particular line in the Holy Book. Or rather, a cluster of separate but thematically related lines and passages, with one line in particular being the absolutely crucial one, determining how the others are interpreted. On its own, and in its immediate context, the line has always been compellingly clear to me. Clear as daylight. And this is something in a book which is often quite obscure, at least to a layman like me, without Arabic (classical or otherwise), and hardly any of the scholarship necessary for a tussle with the Divine Word. Even the verses which are thematically related to that one unambiguous line and could be read as endorsing it, I have difficulty with. The line? "*La ikraha fi'd'din*", meaning 'there is no compulsion in religion' (*al-Baqarah,* verse 256). For some time now I've been meaning to openly shout from the top of the nearest minaret the unambiguity of that seemingly simple line and confront all its possible implications and complications. But I dared not, because my knowledge of Islamic theology is somewhat limited. And I was not exactly enthusiastic over the prospect of getting entangled with the *ulamas*, especially those with the mentality of a *lebai* (village religious functionary).

77

Then I came across, recently, some lines attributed to that fascinating and controversial figure in the history of Islamic mysticism, Al-Hallaj (10th Century AD), regarded with extreme disapproval by the religious establishment of his day as an extreme example of an 'intoxicated Sufi'. (The epithet 'extreme' becomes 'supreme' in the eyes of the al-Halaj's sympathisers and followers.) The lines? "He (God) sees like an enemy but is a friend. I take His judgements very seriously. God says, 'You are not qualified, Hallaj. But *go ahead and say it anyway.*'" (Italics mine, but the *ulamas* are welcome to them.) So in the case of *la ikraha fi'd-din*, I've decided to go ahead and say what I wanted to say anyway. With all due respect to the old adage about a little learning being a dangerous thing, I'm going to stick my neck out - and I hope God the Compassionate won't damn me. Some *very fundamental* issues are involved here which should be confronted without waiting until one has read all the books. (You see, I too am a 'fundamentalist'; in the *truly fundamental* but non-literalist sense - and after my own fashion.) I also happen to believe that 'a little learning' (meaning book knowledge) is not always, or necessarily, 'a dangerous thing'. You'd be surprised how adequate, in certain things, simple intelligence, uncluttered faith, and common sense can be.

Well, we have this Quranic line, "THERE IS NO COMPUL-SION IN RELIGION." (The capitals are mine, and the *ulamas* are more than welcome to them.) There it is. Superbly simple. Stark. Abrupt in its absoluteness. Yes. Think about it. Really think. Use your God-given mind. Meditate on it with the 'eye of your heart' (*'ayn al-qalb'* of the Sufis), not just with the 'eye of your head'. With the 'eye of the heart', you will, *insha allah*, be able to read this Quranic line with a semblance of the Sufi's 'eye of certainty' (*'ayn al-yaqin'*). Now, if the Quran says so categorically that "there is no compulsion in religion", how come there is the law that Muslims who become apostates (*murtad*) should be punished. AND WITH CAPITAL PUNISHMENT TOO? (The capitals are the *ulamas'*, and they keep them.) I'll deal with this question of punishment later. First, let's confront the word *murtad* itself, and see if the orthodox, fundamentalist (in *their* sense) *ulamas* have not, through the ages, invoked the word *murtad* too readily, too rigidly. I want to examine this question with reference to literature. Some time ago, in this column, I wrote about the 'infidel' Mexican poet Octavio Paz's idea of poetry as that mysterious, ambivalent and ambiguous 'other voice'. The passage that is immediately pertinent here, and which I thoroughly endorse, is this: "At one of its extremes, poetry touches the electric border of religious vision ... it has been alternately revolutionary and reactionary ... all its loves have ended in divorce, and all its conversions in apostasy. Poetry has continually been a stubborn intractable heterodoxy; an incessant zig-zagging rebellion against doctrines and churches ... other-worldly and this-wordly ... Heretical and devout, innocent and perverted, limpid and murky." A poet who expresses this heterodoxy need not be an atheist or infidel; there have been major poets in many religious traditions of the world who could remain essentially believers and yet receptive to poetry's 'other voice'. And it is worth thinking about that it is this very heterodoxy that explains poetry's ability, in Paz's words, "to place contrary or divergent realities in relationship ... to seek, and often find, hidden resemblances ... Each poem is (thus) a practical lesson in harmony and concord."

Major Muslim poets and Sufis like (here goes my name dropping) Rumi, al-Halaj, al-Arabi, al-Junayd (a remote 'ancestor' of mine), Hafiz, Omar Khayyam, and certainly that 'blasphemously' forthright and wine-besotted poet of 8th Century Baghdad, Abu Nuwas (in the *Thousand and One Nights*, boon companion of Harun al-Rashid - and my spiritual brother) - all these major figures in Islamic literature were, in varying degrees and in one way or another, blessed with the ability to hear poetry's other voice, and therefore, essentially heterodox. And, being true to that other voice, the work of these poets and their thinking reveals 'hidden resemblances' and affirms 'harmony and concord', and is therefore True (i.e. Divine) Unity that transcends all divisive doctrines and orthodoxies. Or, in other words, they affirm the spiritual brotherhood of (universal) man. Remember Rumi the Sufi and the line about many lamps but only one light? (See *AIP*, Sept 9, 1992) I've always thought that, within Islam, the Sufis understand these things better than the conservative ulamas and ayatolahs. If there is such a thing as the transcendent unity of religions (the title, by the way, of an illuminating book by the Swiss scholar Fritjof Schuon), then the poet would be tempted to argue that, in the most fundamental sense (the only sense that matters?), for a non-atheist, there is no such thing as 'apostasy'. Please kindly note that I said 'tempted', implying that the temptation could be a dangerously satanic one.

Religion and Creative Freedom

[17th November 1993]

Yes, God says: "There is no compulsion in religion." (See my last column.) And yet ...

In 1986 the writer-poet Kassim Ahmad was declared an apostate by the Perak Religious Council for publishing a book highly critical of the Hadith (traditions of the Prophet). The book, which sparked off a heated controversy in the Press, was eventually banned, and Kassim himself received an anonymous death threat for having written it. A similar thing happened in Egypt recently. A noted law professor was declared an apostate because of his critique of strict Islamic law. Fundamentalists even demanded that the courts dissolve his marriage; his being an apostate, it was claimed, had made the marriage illegal. His alleged apostasy had made his wife an adulteress who deserved to be stoned to death. Some militant fundamentalists even take the law into their own hands, assasinating individuals whom they brand as apostates or blasphemers. The shooting of the distinguished Egyptian writer and thinker Farag Foda last year is a very disturbing sign of things to come. Recently the *al-Gamaa al-Islamia* (Islamic Group) announced that the Nobel laureate Naguib Mahfouz, considered disrespectful to Islam, was at the top of its death list. The old writer now moves around with police bodyguards. Egypt has long been known as one of the most liberal of Islamic countries, but it seems to be becoming less so. The militant fundamentalists, who seem to have taken root in many areas of government and institutions, are becoming more influential and dangerous. Even the Al Azhar University - Islam's oldest theology school - is showing signs of being controlled by fundamentalists. It has recently banned some of Mahfouz's novels from its courses, and its Rector has even teamed up with an influential *ulama* (Islamic theologian and jurist) in branding any arguments in favour of the separation of religion and the State as 'apostasy'. In September this year a Bangladeshi woman writer, Taslima Nasreen, had a death sentence pronounced on her for publishing a novella (*Lajja* or *Shame*) about discrimination against religious minorities in

81

her country. This so-called 'fatwa' was not issued by the Bangladeshi equivalent of an ayatolah or the chief *imam* of the state, but by a group of fundamentalist clerics who sought to punish Nasreen for writing books which allegedly "conspire against Islam". The government of Bangladesh has maintained a disturbing silence over this 'fatwa', thus virtually legitimising it.

In a number of Islamic countries, apostasy as well as blasphemy are capital offences. But it's one thing to have such laws, another to actually implement them. A country which definitely implements them is Iran. I believe Pakistan does too, at least it did until Benazir Bhutto was returned to power recently. The Rushdie affair apparently has done a lot in making the Pakistani Government more intransigent in religious matters. Is there any justification for making apostasy a criminal offence? Going by the verse in the Quran about the freedom of faith, there certainly isn't. But the vast majority of *fuqahas* (jurists) maintain otherwise.

A book by a Universiti Kebangsaan Malaysia lecturer in *shariah* (Islamic law) - *Islamic Criminal Law and Criminal Behaviour* (published by ABIM, 1993) - puts the dominant *fuqaha* viewpoint very starkly: "Islam forces every Muslim to be Muslim forever." This viewpoint, embodied in the criminal law code of Islamic states like Iran and Pakistan, is justified by reference to both the Quran and Hadith. It seems that the verse about freedom of faith in Surah *al-Baqarah* is no inconvenience to the orthodox *fuqahas*. They claim that if the verse is read with reference to the historical circumstance of its revelation, it would be clear that 'no compulsion' refers to infidels, not Muslims. In other words, God forbids conversion of infidels, but once a person is a Muslim his renunciation of his faith is a criminal offence punishable by the state. This more or less standard reading of the verse from *al-Baqarah* is reinforced by reference to other related verses of the Quran (such as verse 217 of the same Surah, verse 11-12 of Surah *at-Tawbah*, verse 86-87 of Surah *al-'Imran* and verse 137 of Surah *al-Nisa*). I myself am not convinced that these verses of the Quran really regard apostasy as a criminal offence. It is a sin, and a grave one, yes; but nowhere is it suggested that the apostate-offender as such deserves to be executed. What is implied is divine punishment in the Hereafter. To me, the unambiguity of the emphatic line from *al-Baqarah* is made even more unambiguous by lines like the following: "Whosoever will, let him believe and whosoever will, let him disbelieve." (al-Kahf, 29); "Unto you your religion and unto me my religion." (al-Kafirun, 6) When a particular verse does talk of slaying apostates, the historical occasion of the Revelation must be taken into account. It has to be remembered that in the early years of Islam, when the new religion was struggling to establish itself, persons who defected from it tended to join its enemies and were therefore a threat to it. This means that a distinction must be made between apostate as apostate and apostate as active enemy. The Quran, therefore, specifically guarantees Muslims liberty of belief; any act of apostasy is an afffirmation of that liberty, and therefore shouldn't be punishable - by the state or by any militant fanatic who appoints himself a guardian of the faith, and as guardian appropriates the function of God.

But the dominant orthodox view on apostasy finds its strongest justification not in the Quran but in the Hadith. There are a number of hadiths which are categorical in their rejection of the freedom of belief enshrined in the Quran. The best known one has the Prophet say: "Whosoever changes his religion, cut his head off!" (narrated by Ibn 'Abas). He is also believed to have said: "It is not lawful to shed the blood of a person professing Islam ... except in three cases - when he commits murder, adultery and apostasy." When a hadith is invoked we enter an area that should be fully open to debate but in some countries (like our own) it is not, as the case of Kassim Ahmad showed. Recently there has been much sinister talk by the religious authorities about 'anti-hadith' groups in institutions of higher learning. It seems that 'anti-hadith' is becoming a convenient smear word used by the *ulamas* as readily as the word *murtad* (apostate). My view of the Hadith in relation to the question of apostasy is a simple one. If a hadith, like the two quoted above, contradicts what is unambiguously affirmed in the Quran, then it has to be rejected as unauthentic. Surely it's obvious that the Prophet is unlikely to have uttered anything that contradicts the word of God. As for the poet, he should always listen to the voice of his artistic conscience: that 'other voice' Octavio Paz talks of which affirms unity in diversity and sings the song of concord that transcends conflicts of doctrine. Poetry, like other forms of literature, can only perform its proper function in a state of creative freedom. There shouldn't be any

83

compulsion in poetry as there shouldn't be any in religion. Given the transcendent unity of religions, what the jealous guardians of orthodoxy too readily call 'apostasy' may only be the healthy exercise of that creative freedom sanctioned by God Himself.

Apostates of the World, Rejoice!

[12th February 1992]

The Sunday before last (Feb 2) was the birthday of the great Irish novelist James Joyce (born 1882). I'd like to use the occasion to talk about him, to celebrate him as an example to a certain kind of writer caught in a certain kind of situation. Joyce is a perfect example of the writer fully attuned to 'the other voice' of his art. The voice that, to echo the words of the Mexican poet Octavio Paz, is stubbornly and intractably heterodox, whose loves have always ended in divorce, whose conversions in apostasy. Joyce is, in fact, the prototype of the modern artist as apostate. His apostasy, both literal and symbolic, cultural, political as well as religious, was inseparable from the integrity of his vision, and the freedom of his art. It led him into self-exile; almost his entire adult life was spent wandering from one European country to another. He died and was buried in Zurich on Jan 13, 1941. Like all true writers who felt compelled to revolt, Joyce's apostasy and self-exile were, ironically, his means of affirming his essential 'Irishness', of being true to the real heritage of his race. But his fidelity was totally unlike that of the blinkered and puritanical nationalists. It was open to life in all its richness and contradictions, embracing with the human breadth of its art the Irish and the non-Irish, the local and the universal, the vulgar and the refined, the profane and the sacred. Joyce had to say No (and No, in thunder) in order to truly rejoice in the saying of Yes - the great Yes of Molly Bloom as she sits on the chamber-pot at the end of *Ulysses*. And, to quote one of the sharpest early commentators on Joyce, he, by means of his art, "proves himself most truly a Catholic, even if he could only exhibit the Catholic temper by rejecting the Catholic faith, as he knew it".

While still a young man, Joyce made himself the champion in Ireland of the Norwegian playwright Henrik Ibsen, then an old man with his last play, *When We Dead Awaken*, already behind him. Ibsen's hatred of ultra-nationalism, dead conventions and provincialism made him Joyce's spiritual relation. It was typical of Joyce's countrymen that his passionate championing of the foreign playwright was considered unpatriotic as well as anti-religious, the latter really meaning anti the Catholic Church which had the mind of Ireland in its vice-like grip. Provincialism, puritanism, religious fanaticism, and nationalism lost in the fog and bog of sheer Irish sentimentality - all this had made Joyce's beloved native city Dublin, that one-time centre of European learning and culture, a 'centre of paralysis'.It was in order to look hard and with the detachment of estrangement at this 'centre of paralysis' that Joyce exiled himself. Sensitive to 'the other voice', he knew that his love must end in divorce, his faith in apostasy. But that same voice, heterodox with the heterodoxy of both life and art, led him to the recovery of true love - or rather a reaffir-mation of love enlarged by the human breadth of his art.

In his greatest work, *Ulysses*, set in Dublin with a'dirty-minded' common man (a Jew too, not an Irishman) as its true hero, he traces step by earth-bound step his way through the labyrinth of the city's provincial streets and alleys towards the great affirmation. Someone, with Joyce's final work *Finnegans Wake* in mind, once nicely said of Joyce, "he had the Liffey water in his veins and on his brain; the river whose name puns so naturally with the water of life". By putting and immortalising Dublin on the literary map of the world, the arrogant 'traitor' with nothing but contempt for the noisy patriotic mob became the greatest celebrant of the native city on which he had turned his back for good. As Stephen Daedalus, the hero of Joyce's autobiographical novel *A Portrait of the Artist as a Young Man*, puts it on the eve of his own exile: "The shortest way to Tara (is) via Holyhead." (Tara is the ancient seat of the Kings of Ireland until the 6th Century and here symbolises the past glory of Irish civilisation; Holyhead, the coastal town in northern Wales, is the landing point of the ferry from Dublin.)

The writer Sean O'Faolain, a true patriot (he was for six years a member of the Irish Republican Army) and yet as unblinkered by sentimentalism as Joyce was, once suggested expatriation or self-exile as one of the major reasons for the flowering of Anglo-Irish literature early this century. "The intellectual blood transfusion" resulting from this tradition of literary expatriation was in part due to the fact that most Irish writers simply couldn't forget their bloody country wherever they might have exiled themselves. O'Faolain gave another reason for that flowering of Anglo-Irish literature which I should perhaps quote here - and that was "the imposition on Gaelic Ireland of the English language and the example of its masterpieces, the one offering the Irish writers access to the widest audience and the other access to a thousand shades of style". Joyce himself never had any feeling of guilt in having to use the language of Ireland's colonial masters, and he had nothing but scorn for the movement to revive a dead language like Gaelic.

In invoking James Joyce the self-exiled apostate as an example, I don't mean to recommend emigration to those of our writers who feel that they are in a situation in this country akin to that of the Irishman in his. It is Joyce's fierce fidelity to his vision and his uncompromising sense of artistic integrity that I mean to stress. Joyce felt the need to exile himself, and his exile proved to be a fruitful one, yes. But that doesn't mean every writer in a situation akin to Joyce's must necessarily emigrate if he doesn't want to die as a writer. It must be remembered that exile can take more than one form; it doesn't have to be physical. There is such a thing as internal or spiritual exile, a form that some noted writers of the world have resorted to. In his column *Other Cadences* (Literary Page, Jan 8), Wong Phui Nam raised a challenging question about emigration. The question he raised has a special reference to writers who feel that they have "no place in the new order of things". The words within quotation marks were those of the Malacca-born poet Ee Tiang Hong who emigrated to Australia and died there a few years ago. In fact, it was the case of Ee Tiang Hong, as seen by his friend and fellow poet Edwin Thumboo in a poem addressed to him, that occasioned the question raised by Mr Wong. Without mincing his words, Mr Wong says that "emigration is an evasion, a lack of will to come to terms with one's condition". Though his interesting reading of Thumboo's poem is invoked in support of that statement, the wording makes it sound absolute, which I'm quite sure was not intended by Mr Wong. Is emigration - especially that of a writer - always "an evasion, a lack of will to come to terms with one's condition"? The striking case of Joyce alone should make Mr Wong want to qualify his statement. Mr Wong also believes that Ee's emigration was a sad one because it was really a quest for 'elusive Edens' that landed him in a desert of the mind. And Mr Wong here invokes his reading of Thumboo's poem in support of his judgement. I too think that there was a certain sadness in Ee's emigration, but I'm not sure about the 'desert' bit. Ee Tiang Hong's case is interesting and an unsentimental discussion of it could generate some insights into the question of emigration as a temptation facing certain kinds of writers in this country. Though understated, the special reference of the question raised by Mr Wong is obviously to those English-language non-Bumi writers who feel that they have "no place in the new order of things".

Without suggesting that Mr Wong is unaware of it, I would like to remind non-Bumis that even a Bumi writer, if he can hear 'the other voice' of his art, or if his art is capable of 'the other voice', can feel that he has 'no place in the new order of things' and because of it can face the temptation of self-exile. In one sense, the tempatation can even be stronger because the Bumi writer of the kind I mean has to suffer from worse constraints on his creative freedom than the non-Bumi, despite all the talk of his being a member of a privileged race. For reasons which I don't have space to go into here, I believe that physical exile for this Bumi writer could be the death of his creativity. If James Joyce the defiant apostate must serve as an example to him, it has to be a symbolic one. His exile must be internal or spiritual - and if he has the resources and the strength to bear with that condition and even turn it into a creative blessing, there is no reason why he can't rejoice in his 'apostasy' - with the Joycean line "silence, exile and cunning" for a motto - the 'silence' here meaning the cunningly articulate 'silence' of art. Whether his rejoicing as expressed in his art can be shared by his countrymen, whether the 'silence' will in fact be a public one, is, of course, another matter.

On Not Going the Whole Hog

[28th February 1991 and 3rd April 1991]

The Rushdie Affair has long ceased to dominate the headlines. But it is not quite over yet, despite the apostate author's surprising 'conversion' last December (1990). Only the other day, I heard *The Satanic Verses* being mentioned in a BBC news item about the thorny issue of a British hostage in Lebanon. It seems that the Ayatollah's pronouncement regarding Rushdie's 'conversion', that it made no difference to the so-called *fatwa* on his life, still stands. I put 'conversion' within inverted commas because I don't think it's the right word for it. I am not trying to be an amateur *mujtahid* (religious scholar), but I think they all have got it wrong about this latest turn of events in the saga of the Rushdie scandal. Pardon me if *I* am wrong, but since Salman Rushdie was born into a Bombay Muslim family, his return to the faith of his ancestors after his apostasy should be considered just that - a return. What is required in such cases, according to Islamic law as I understand it, is the performance (sic) of a public *tawba* (repentance) by the author. As I understand it (forgive me, *ustaz* (religious teacher), if I am again wrong), Allah is All-Merciful and is ever willing to welcome the apostate back into the fold of true believers. (Man it seems, even an Ayatollah, is less generous.) Whether the performance of the *tawba* is just a 'performance' in the sense of being a mere show, a piece of theatre for the benefit of those millions thirsting for the apostate's blood, it is not up to other Muslims to judge. What's really in the heart and mind of the self-declared repentant apostate only Allah the All-Knowing knows.

In the Rushdie Saga, there have been so many ironies that even a writer of Rushdie's brilliance as spinner of phantasmagorical tales can be stunned. (God is indeed the greatest novelist, the mightiest 'magic realist' of them all.) We can start with the man's very name: Salman, which means 'the saved', 'the tranquil and happy one', is the name of the first Persian convert to Islam (perhaps this ironic coincidence was the real spark that ignited the rage of

Iran's spiritual leader). This Salman El-Farsi (a Zoroastrian before his conversion) is considered by Muslims as the ideal type of seeker after Truth; after he had found it in Islam, he became the ideal type of convert and devoted slave of Allah. As for our novelist's surname, Rushdie, it means 'intelligence, sensibleness, cleverness'. The abundance of ironic coincidences in the whole 'satanic affair' is such that I am tempted to organise my relections on it around that ill-fated name. Salman Rushdie, brilliant novelist and tale spinner, winner of the coveted Booker Prize, is in my considered opinion a clever mind who became a victim of his own cleverness. The devilishly brilliant satire that he used to expose what he saw as contradictions and ambiguities in the image of the much-revered Prophet has led him into the phantasmagoric (more bizarre than his fictions, but real, bloody real) labyrinth of death-in-life. Ayatollah Khomeini's death sentence on him was the patriarch's way of "killing him in such a way as he had never yet killed anyone", as Caliph Harun ar-Rashid (786-809) was recorded to have said about a certain *Mut'azilite* (rationalist theologian) who dared to claim that the Quran was created.

It was no use (as subsequent events proved) for Rushdie and his defenders to say that *The Satanic Verses* was fiction. It was equally useless even to argue that properly read, with a sensibility schooled in the pyrotechnics of post-modernist 'magic realism', the novel, however satirically funny in parts, was thematically a serious and essentially responsible piece of work; and that even the portrait of Mahound (Muhammad), despite passages that sounded offensive out of context, could not be considered *gratuitously* 'blasphemous'. This kind of argument would have made sense if Rushdie and his defenders were dealing with literary critics or readers educated in literature, especially in the aesthetics of the Western post-modernist novel. But once the work had been dragged into the maelstrom of religious passions, no appeal to literary values could have had any effect. And so it turned out. It was revealing that even Muslim intellectuals fairly adequately educated in the modern novel reacted in rage to the work. And it was even more revealing, and I would say disturbingly so, that there were fairly distinguished local minds (columnists with a name) who denounced the novel obviously without having read it, except probably the specifically offensive extracts that were circulating around. The rage provoked by *The Satanic Verses* was truly and tragically beyond belief. Almost. For this the author himself, I am afraid, was largely to be blamed. The novel would not have made the headlines that led to violent protests from Bradford to Bangladesh in which many lives were lost, if Rushdie himself had not helped to make it happen. In a sense Rushdie knew what he was doing when he wrote the novel in the manner he did, and promoted it in the way he did - but he disastrously miscalculated the extent of the risks he was consciously taking.

As I see it, two things brought to the fore by the affair should be given serious thought by writers cursed by a creative compulsion to be recklessly 'blasphemous'. I am thinking especially of writers living in the West who originally came from a taboo culture and are still considered part of it or connected with it, even though they are now exiles or 'apostates' from that culture. The two things are the temptations of superstardom offered to the serious writer by the present-day world of high-pressure publishing; and, related to the first, the phenomenon of the writer as media performer. Rushdie as a novelist makes me green with envy. But as literary superstar who exploited and was in turn exploited by the mega-business of publishing, he is not a model to be emulated. The confidential memos from inside Viking Penguin (Rushdie's publisher), leaked to the press, revealed highly dubious pressures other than strictly literary that worked on him and his publishers, and helped to ensure that the yet-to-be published novel would be treated as a hot media event rather than literature. In promoting the novel, Rushdie couldn't resist the temptation to play the media monkey, drawing the attention of the masses to himself and the highly explosive work that not many would have heard of, and even less would have read or been capable of reading.

I can't forget the picture of smug Salman with his grinning face, his shiny bald pate reflecting the flashes of a hundred cameras, his low-slung eyelids frozen in the flare of hubris, arms thrown back in triumph, waving a cheque for the biggest advance ever given for a novel. In that moment of triumph before the buzzing paparazzi, Rushdie truly lived up to the meaning of his name ('See, what a clever chap I am!'). Enviable as a novelist, yes, but not when he lets himself be too clever by half to the extent of forgetting something that he, as an Indian-born Muslim and a student of Islamic history, must have known - and that is the extraordinarily deep-seated veneration in which the name and memory of the Prophet is held by Muslims, especially those of the Indian sub-continent and their immigrant brothers in England. One has only to read, for example, Annemarie Schimmel's important study *And Muhammad Is His Messenger: The Veneration of the Prophet in Islamic Piety* (1985) to realise the manner in which Indian and Pakistani Muslims venerate the memory and the 'myth' of the Prophet; this tradition of veneration virtually making Muhammad semi-divine. It has been said that with the Indian and Pakistani Muslims, you can get away with insulting God, but not the Beloved Prophet.

If Rushdie had not in his excess of cleverness forgotten this simple fact, he, with his amazing resources as a novelist, would have found a different way of handling the historical basis of his fiction. He could, in particular, have given the portrait of Mahound/Muhammad a different kind of treatment without sacrificing the essense of his theme and vision. He could for example have considered the wisdom of resorting to subtlety of tones and ambiguity of language; and not naively assume that his pious Muslim reader, at least the educated ones, would understand and accept the dramatic principle of fiction (that, for example, when in the novel Baal, the pagan poet, calls Mahound/ Muhammad a "bastard", or Salman the prophet's scribe is made to say he believes his boss and leader to be a "conjurer", it doesn't mean they are speaking for the author). "Tell the truth, but tell it slant," said Emily Dickinson; if Rushdie had remembered this when he decided to tell his 'truth' about such a sensitive subject as Muhammad, he might have reduced the possibility of his novel being misunderstood or distorted by uncomprehending fundamentalist demagogues and literalists. Rushdie, after all, isn't the first Muslim-born author to be accused of blasphemy. In this century, the most notable case is probably the Nobel laureate Naguib Mahfouz whose 1959 novel *The Children of Gebelaawi* created a furore in Egypt when it was serialized in the national daily *Al Ahram*. But the Mahfouz who wrote the offending novel wasn't a Rushdie subjected to the temptations of modern Western publishing practice and the seduction of the media monster. And the Egyptian, I gather, wasn't blessed (or cursed) by the talent of recklessly brilliant provocative satire on sacred subjects. (It is interesting to note that Mahfouz defended Rushdie at first, even before reading the latter's novel, but after reading the novel and the threats to his own life for defending the blasphemer, he changed his mind.) And now, after nearly two years in hiding from the long arm of Ayatollah, the literary superstar was finally compelled to capitulate. The defiant stance in the sacred name of artistic freedom and integrity had to be abandoned finally, much to the disappointment of his defenders who felt their hero had let them down. Was Rushdie's so-called 'conversion' genuine? We don't know, and probably won't know.

Many Indian Muslims of Bradford and Manchester (like that grimly uncompromising, unforgiving pro-Iranian head of the Muslim Institute, Dr Kalim Siddiqui), thought Rushdie's repentant return to the fold was a hyprocritical act of a cornered man. Desperation or sheer mortal terror was obviously a crucial factor, but we cannot really discount the possibility of mortal terror, by some mysterious metamorphosis of the spirit, suddenly slashing a slit in Rushdie's secular armour, letting in the Light of lights. Sometime last January, I heard on the BBC Overseas Service an interview with Dr Zaki Badawi, principal of the Muslim College in London. In that interview extracts from an earlier interview with the newly 'converted' Rushdie were replayed and commented on by both the interviewer and Dr Badawi. This was how parts of the interview, and the interview-within-the-interview, went:

Interviewer (*to Rushdie in the earlier interview*): Will this (your conversion) mean in the most basic terms that you will give up alcohol and pray five times a day?

Rushdie: Uh ... Well ... I don't have to do ... Uh ... everything .... Uh ... As I said, I'm still an extremely bad Muslim ... What I said to them is, you'll have to permit me to find my route towards it in my own way ...

Interviewer: Dr Badawi, does that sound like a man who has totally embraced Islam?

Dr Badawi: ... the ordinary Muslim would expect a convert to be more than that ... I think that might raise some doubt about Mr Rushdie's conversion ... However, one hopes that this is the first step .... that Mr Rushdie will move quickly and effectively towards observing all the tenets of Islam ...

Interviewer: You're saying he hasn't gone the whole hog then?...

Was that - the 'going the whole hog' bit, I mean - a piece of BBC witticism? More likely it's a Freudian slip. I can imagine Rushdie's disappointed supporters saying: "Yes, Mr BBC, how right you are. Our hero has indeed failed to go the whole hog." Rushdie said something else in the interview which made me less reluctant to take his 'conversion' as one of those mysterious but authentic things that can happen to people in his bizzare situation. He said: "If I were dishonest with myself about this (the conversion), it would destroy my life as a writer ... If one is not entirely truthful with oneself, when one sits down to create a work of art, it becomes a dishonest work of art ... Therefore, if I were saying something here which I could not live with, which I did not in my heart accept, it would be impossible for me to continue my work, and the most important thing in my life is my work ..." The BBC man, who had earlier committed a forbidden Freudian slip, at this point made what I can only describe as an asinine comment addressed to Dr Badawi. He said: "Now there's a man who claims that he has been converted to Islam and yet his work is the most important thing to him. How do you react to that, Dr Badawi?" A power failure, caused I think by a sudden lightning strike, out of the blue almost, cut short my reception of the BBC broadcast, and I didn't get to hear Dr Badawi's reply to the ass's question.

But for your benefit, dear reader, I'll give what I think is the only answer an intelligent man can give. When a writer says that his work is the most important thing in his life, it doesn't mean God is less important. How could He be? Isn't God beyond comparison? Certainly with anything as mortal as the creations of the creature He had, in His Boundless Incomparable Magnanimity created - one named, with prophetic irony, Salman Rushdie.

Speaking Up for a Writer's Right

[15th December 1993]

The 'scimitar' of Khomeini, sharp as the *sirat* bridge over the fires of hell, still 'hangs' from beyond the grave, by a mere slice of a hair, over poor Rushdie's balding head. It's almost five years now since that notorious Iranian *fatwa*. Five long dark years. The scimitar above - and before him - stretches the blindingly tempting prospect of his own immortality. Immortal in name, I mean - Salman Rushdie, famous (or infamous) the world over till the end of time. During one of his rare forays into the glare of public notice, in Norway a few months ago, Rushdie talked about his exile-in-limbo as some sort of blessing in disguise. It had given him, he said, the "chance to talk about hugely important values"; a chance which he considered a "privilege". "When you face an issue of life and death," he went on, "it makes you see what's important. You cut away all the frippery of life. It clarifies you."

"Clarifies" him? Which 'him'? Himself as an individual caught between two cultures? As a rootless post-modernist writer? A voice of modern migrant man condemned to existential hybridity? Or simply as a two-time apostate turned into that hybrid of hybrids - a 'secular Muslim', whatever that means? How the whole sorry business has 'clarified' Salman the deracinated Muslim-born Indian, God only knows. It'll no doubt be clarified in the book he is planning to write about his unique experience of the last five terrible years. Meanwhile, he said, thanks to the Ayatollah (may Allah have mercy on his soul), he had "more friends now than in 1989". Until recently, these new 'friends' of his, at least the publically known ones, were mainly infidel Westerners whom Muslims had no difficulty in dismissing as 'enemies' of Islam. (Including the latest 'friend', the infidel bigwig Clinton?) 'Enemies' who no doubt loved 'Salman Sambo', for 'proving' their worst suppositions about that religion of 'barbaric' rage called *Submission*.

Until recently, I said. Because last month there unexpectedly appeared in Paris a book called *For Rushdie* in which one hundred

Arab and Muslim writers and intellectuals from "a dozen Muslim countries" declared their solidarity with the beleaguered apostate. Big names like the Egyptian Nobel laureate Naguib Mahfouz, distinguished Moroccan novelist Tahar Ben Jelloun, the brilliant Syrian-born Lebanese poet Adonis (pen name of Ali Ahmed Said), and the prominent Palestinian scholar-intellectual Edward Said - they all defended, in one big chorus of a hundred voices, Rushdie's fundamental right as writer. Specifically, the right to publish *The Satanic Verses*, however much they may have disagreed with the way he had exercised that right, and even if they painfully agreed that it was a work of reckless blasphemy. Mahfouz's name among the hundred is the least surprising, since this old man has been seen by Egyptian fundamentalists as a "Rushdie before Rushdie". And his 1959 novel *Children of Gebelaawi,* which he called "my illegitimate son" and is regarded by some as a sort of half-formed 'precursor' of *The Satanic Verses*, had earned him a top place in the fundamentalists' hit list. Mahfouz was reported as saying in the book *For Rushdie*: "The veritable terrorism of which Rushdie is a target is unjustifiable, indefensible ... One idea can only be opposed by other ideas. Even if the punishment is carried out, the idea as well as the book will remain." Right, Mahfouz! The other Muslim writer, Tahar Ben Jelloun, is the author of the 1987 Prix Goncourt winner, that allegedly "impious pornographic" novel *La Nuit Sacree* (The Sacred Night), which (believe me or not) has actually been translated into Malay. Called *Malam Kudus*, it was published by Dewan Bahasa dan Pustaka early this year and, soon after its semi-absurdist launching by our Royal 'Renaissance-Man' Professor, was silently withdrawn or in effect banned. Ben Jelloun was reported as saying in the book *For Rushdie* that "no matter how much offence Rushdie's book might have caused, to condemn him to death for what he wrote was intolerable and has nothing to do with the tolerant Islam that I was taught." Good on you, Ben J!

The other one of the daring hundred, Edward Said, is not a Muslim. A Palestinian Christian-born self-confessed secularist, Said is widely known as the author of four highly important books: *The Question of Palestine, Orientalism, Covering Islam,* and most recently, *Culture and Imperialism* - all of which are eloquent testimonies to his deep sympathy with the Arab-Islamic world, as well as his hawk-eyed perceptiveness into the hidden evils of Western 'cultural imperialism' in all its forms. Edward Said has a moving piece in *The Rushdie File* (edited by Lisa Appignanesi and Sara Maitland, ICA Fourth Estate, 1989) where he makes a very forceful point that should be heeded by all true writers from the Islamic world, with whom Said, though a non-Muslim, identifies himself. "We cannot accept," says Said, "the notion that democratic freedom should be abrogated to protect Islam."

Islam, he implies, is strong enough to be able to tolerate freedom of expression, within and beyond its realm, however 'offensive' the exercise of that freedom may be, as long as the 'offensiveness' is not gratuitous or mindlessly irresponsible (the only limits to this freedom that can be accepted by true writers). What Said says in reference to the Rushdie case in particular deserves to be quoted at some length. From his position as Professor of English and Comparative Literature in a citadel of Western scholarship (Columbia University), Said says: "*The Satanic Verses* is an astonishing and prodigiously inventive work of fiction ... It is, in all sorts of ways, a deliberately trangressive work ...(written) with bold, nose-thumbing, post-modern daring. And in so doing it demonstrates another side of its author's unbroken engagement with the politics and history of the contemporary scene. Salman Rushdie is after all the same distinguished writer and intellectual who has spoken out for immigrants', black and Palestinian rights, against imperialism and racialism." (Thanks, Professor Said, for this reminder; too many of our Muslim *mindas* (minds), name-dropping pseudos and compulsive riders of the latest ideological *kereta lembu* (bullock cart), have short memories - or simply don't bloody know what's actually what.) While acknowledging and feeling an empathy with the hurt and anguish felt by Muslims about Rushdie's novel, its irreverence and 'blasphemies', Said tries to see the whole tragic business from the viewpoint of those angry offended Muslims. He says: "Most Moslems think of the situation between their community and Western civilisation in singularly unhappy terms. How many Islamic writers ... are published, much less known or read, in the West? And why is that ignorance there, if not for the disregard, indifference and fear with which things Islamic are considered here (the West)? ... "Islam," he continues, "is reduced to terrorism and fundamentalism and now, alas, is seen to be acting accordingly, in

97

the ghastly violence prescribed by Ayatollah Khomeini. The fury increases as do the pieties and the vindictive righteousness. Above all, however, there rises the question that people from the Islamic world ask: Why must a Moslem (meaning someone like Rushdie), who could be defending and sympathetically interpreting us, now represent us so roughly, so expertly and so disrespectfully to an audience already primed to excoriate our traditions, reality, history, religion, language and origin? Why, in other words, must a member of our culture join the legions of Orientalists in Orientalizing Islam so radically and unfairly?" Acknowledging "the anguish and seriousness" in these questions, questions which demand to be answered, Said suggests something that we should listen to carefully. Says Said, the contemporary world being one, even with its many spheres and divisions, and Salman Rushdie, being both "in this world" and "from the community of Islam", has written for the West about Islam. *The Satanic Verses* thus is a *self-representation* (italics mine). But everyone should be able to read the novel, interpret it, understand, accept, or finally reject it. And more to the point it should be possible both to accept (the novel's) brilliance and also to note its transgressive apostasy." It's a "peculiar paradox", continues Said, and "also an emblem of the fate of hybrids and immigrants (like Rushdie himself)", a fate which is also "part of this contemporary world. For the point is that there is no pure, unsullied, unmixed essence to which some of us can return ... Rushdie's work is not just *about* the mixture, it *is* that mixture itself. To stir Islamic narrative into a stream of heterogeneous narratives about actors, trickers, prophets, devils, whores, heroes, heroines is therefore inevitable ... " Said's is the most perceptive reading of *The Satanic Verses* that I know of; and coming from someone like him, not an intellectual 'Uncle Tom' or a 'Said Sambo', but the most subversive critic of Orientalism, his are words to which modern Muslim writers should at least give a careful hearing. It is no endorsement of Rushdie's "blasphemy", intended or unintended, to agree with Said, Ben Jelloun or Malfouz.

Believe me, I've agonised much about the matter. In my *khalwats* (retreats) from the literary world, I've even had nightmarish visions of that scimitar-shaped *sirat* above my own poor balding head; quite a big head, but not one tenth as big as Rushdie's. That scimitar - and of course, the furnace of damnation ... Even after all this, I can't honestly say I disagree with Edward Said, Ben Jelloun and Mahfouz. I still stand by what I have said in this column about Rushdie and that terrible 'mistake' called *The Satanic Verses* (see *AIP*, April 1991). I blamed Rushdie in part then for the tragic consequence of the recklessly brilliant 'mistake', and I still do. Now, assured somewhat by those hundred voices of solidarity in the name of intelligence and creative freedom, I must do what I've long meant to do. To squeak my teeny and much sullied Muslim voice, for what it's worth, in clear affirmation of that necessary freedom.

In the name of what's truly glorious, tolerant and humane in the heritage of Islam as I know it, it's time the colossal fatuity of the so-called *fatwa* be seen by all true Muslim writers for what it is: a presumptuous, blasphemously un-Islamic, terroristic utterance, against the grain of our religion and our humanity, not to say of international law. It's time that we Muslim writers and intellectuals articulated our dissent from the 'Islam' the fundamentalists would want to impose on us. Surely, it is no way to fight the gross misconceptions of Islam by Western media and scholarship by screaming for the blood of unorthodox writers and alleged apostates. Allah the All Knowing, All Merciful, who says in the Quran that "there is no compulsion in religion", would, I'm quite sure agree with me. At least that's what my 'gut sense' of faith tells me. La ilaha illallah, Muhammadur rasulullah. Allahu Akbar!

The Murder of a Poet

[1st May 1991]

I read a book over the *Hari Raya* (End of *Ramadan* Festival) break which affected me deeply, stirring up old concerns about the hazardous business of being a certain kind of writer in a certain kind of society. The kind of writer I have in mind is not, as you might think, one who is ideologically committed or fired by topical issues that prick his social conscience and because of that gets into conflict with a repressive State. The writer I am thinking of is one whose very stance as a writer and as as individual and the values that inform his non-topical writings and his unconventional lifestyle constitute a challenge, not so much to the State but to society at large. I am thinking of the writer who cherishes an open mind (and heart), and that mere openness - openness to life basically - is an offence to his society. The society in question may on the surface look modern and open but in reality is still ruled by group taboos, ancient prejudices and life-denying pieties.

The book that set me thinking again about this old problem may seem remote, both in terms of geography and time. It is a biography of a Spanish poet and playwright who died more than half a century ago. But if you believe as I do that history can repeat itself, in different situations, different cultures, but with a familiar pattern of conflict underlying them, you might consider the tragic story of this poet not so irrelevant to us. The poet, Frederico Garcia Lorca, was brutally murdered near his hometown of Granada at the beginning of the Spanish Civil War between the Nationalist (read Fascist) rebels and the Republican government in 1936. He was then only 38 and at the height of his powers as a poet and playwright. His murderers were Fascist thugs who took advantage of the chaos of the early days of the civil war to settle old scores with the poet they hated so much. During the civil war, which ended with the victory of the Nationalists under General Franco in 1939, the name of the murdered poet became a powerful political symbol of the Left. And it was used by cynical Communist propogandists to exploit the idealism of progressive writers the world over. The myth of Lorca as a martyr of Communism has long been exploded. But the idea that he was nevertheless an example of the politically committed writer who had to pay with his life for his commitment seems to persist, especially among people who have neither read his writing nor know much about his life.

That the case of Lorca is more complicated, and more disturbing, is shown by the new biography by Ian Gibson (Faber paperback, 1990). The picture of the poet that emerges from this superb book is that of a man who was inspired by an exuberant lust for life yet haunted by an obsession with death. The two sides of his self were rooted in the ambivalence of his heritage and his equally ambivalent attitude to it. Ambivalence and paradox, in fact, seem to run right through the life and work of this Andulusian prodigy. He was one of the most regional of Spanish writers, rooted to the soil of Andulusia, its blood and mire, songs of joy and laments of despair, and yet universal in his appeal. In form, he was both traditional and modern, rooted to the ballads and folk music of the peasants and the Gypsies, but also open to the avant-garde influence of the day (he was a close friend and early collaborator of Salvador Dali). Lorca's universalism is not the sort much cared for by ideologues. His universalism has to do with the primitive yearnings of humanity, the desires of the spirit and the flesh, and the tragic consequences of the denial or betrayal of those desires. The oppression that he was deeply concerned with was not so much political or economic oppression (though he was not unmindful of these), but the oppression of healthy human instincts by a society ruled by a life-denying religious orthodoxy and grimly patriachal values and codes of conduct. Just as Lorca was a true son of Spain who hated the narrow and sterile patriotism of the bourgeoisie and the Nationalists, he was a true if unorthodox Christian who hated the corrupt and repressive Church. In their turn, the Church and the Nationalists, cheerless guardians of the national soul, and the national honour, considered minds like Lorca a corrupting 'cosmopolitan' or 'alien' influence that must be exterminated at all costs. After the myth of Lorca as a martyr of Communism had been exploded, the actual circumstances of and the real reasons for his murder became a subject for speculation.

For a long time, because of the taboo on the poet's name imposed by the Franco regime, it was difficult to establish what actually happened in Granada during those chaotic early days of the civil war. Ian Gibson, author of an earlier study of the murder (banned by the Franco regime), has now in this full length biography placed the tragic event in the context of the poet's whole life and of the Spanish society of his time. We are as a result in a better position to understand the deep-seated as well as the immediate reasons why Lorca was murdered. Lorca may not have been a political writer in the commonly understood sense of the term. But he was even more 'subversive' than the most radical of political writers. Lorca was 'subversive' because he was the voice of primal energies which questioned the repressive orthodoxies of his society and religion, both in the realms of the body and the spirit. "As for me," he was recorded to have said, "I'll never be political. I'm a revolutionary, because all true poets are revolutionaries." What he meant by 'revolutionary' could be inferred from another remark: "The day we stop resisting our instincts, we'll have learnt how to live." His openness to life and all its possibilities meant among other things being a human being first, a Spaniard and a Catholic second. "I am totally Spanish," he said, "and it would be impossible for me to live outside my geographical boundaries. But at the same time, I hate anyone who is Spanish just because he was born a Spaniard. I am a brother to all men, and I detest the person who sacrifices himself for an abstract nationalist and religious ideal ... "

He was outspoken, at times to the point of recklessness. He made many enemies among the religious and nationalist philistines of Granada, and he became a marked man. About two months before they killed him, he made a remark in a newspaper interview that dramatised his ability to rise above the barriers of narrow sentimental patriotism, but which infuriated many Catholic patriots. Asked for his opinion on the fall of Moorish Granada to Ferdinand and Isabella in 1492, he said provocatively: "It was a disastrous event, even though they may say the opposite in the schools. An admirable civilisation, and a poetry, architecture and sensitivity unique in the world - all were lost, to give way to an improverished, cowed city, a 'miser's paradise' where the worst middle class in Spain today is busy stirring things up." The myth of 'the great Christian victory over paganism', so sacred to the chauvinistic Catholic, was dismissed just like that! If there was one remark that sealed Lorca's fate, it must have been this one.

Oh, yes, I almost forgot one other reason why the poet was murdered. He was a homosexual, and we know what being a homosexual was like in a macho, rigidly patriarchal society like Lorca's Spain. One of the thugs who shot him actually boasted that he fired "two bullets into his arse for being a queer". As Gibson grimly comments: "Such was the mentality of the Granada bourgeoisie criticised by the poet (in the newspaper interview quoted above)." And it was tragically fitting that they butchered him at a spot outside Granada not far from a famous fountain once called, by the Arabs, *Ainadamar* (The Fountain of Tears).

1492 and All That ...

(15 April 1992)

Last month, Gapena (National Union of Writers' Associations), in collaboration with *Lembaga Bahasa Melayu Melaka* (Malacca Malay Language Association), held a two-day seminar to commemorate the 500th aniversary of the fall of Granada.

The fall of what?

Granada. You know, the Spanish City - the Alhambra and all that. It was the last bastion of Islamic power in Spain, in case you didn't know, or have forgotten. It fell to the Catholic forces of King Ferdinand and Queen Isabella in 1492. To Muslims, 1492 was a black year; to the Malays it's as black as 1511, when Melaka, the then dominant Islamic power in the East, fell to another Catholic power, Portugal. The parallel is made more striking and galling by the fact that Spain actually succeeded in not only conquering but making Catholics of the Filipinos, a race of people related to the Malays.

The Gapena seminar was the first of a series on the theme *Dunia Melayu, Dunia Islam* (The Malay World, The Muslim World). I didn't attend it, but from reports in the papers I learnt that the topic was 'The Influence of Andalusia (Islamic Spain or al-Andalus) on the Malay World'. The forum that concluded the seminar discussed the effects of the fall of Granada on the Islamic world and the lessons to be learnt by resurgent Islam from that tragic event. Given the tension in relations between the Islamic world and the West today, it is understandable that events like the fall of Granada 500 years ago are so important in the consciousness of resurgent Islam. The tragedy of Bosnia, which has made the Malay poets very vocal, only serves to reinforce old resentments and reopen ancient wounds. But, I hope, when Muslims recall the glory of Islamic civilisations in the remote past, they will do so with more than just sentiment. I hope they will do their homework properly and not merely indulge in pious nostalgia, dropping names like Ibn Rushd (Averroes, to the West) or Abn Arabi without really knowing what those remarkable Muslim minds really stood for.

That al-Andalus (711-1492 A.D.) was a remarkable chapter in Islamic history is uncontestable - even by the infidels, those 'immortal enemies' of Islam. The most moving modern testimony to the glory of Islamic civilisation in Spain that I know of is by a Spanish poet, Federico Garcia Lorca (1898-1936). Lorca, who was born in the Vega (fertile plain) of Granada and was murdered just outside the city by fascist thugs during the Spanish Civil War, was a true spiritual child of al-Andalus. I have written about this marvellous poet in this column (see *The Murder of a Poet*, *AIP*, May 1, 1991), but I think, in this anniversary year of the fall of Granada, it's worth recalling what Muslim Spain meant to this infidel poet and why I believe he should be an example to our own writers. Lorca was distinguished by, among other things, an openness to life and all its possibilities. For him this meant that it was important he was a human being first, a Spaniard and a Catholic second. [1] Lorca was outspoken, at times recklessly so. He was much hated by the Catholic and nationalist philistines of Granada, who later took advantage of the chaos of the civil war to kill him in cold blood. About two months before the murder, he made a remark in a newspaper interview that showed his ability to rise above the barriers of rigid religiosity and sentimental patriotism. [2] I wonder how many of our writers, if they found themselves in a similar historical situation, could be as objective as Lorca is here. I think it could be said that Lorca's cherished universalism was part of an inheritance that included the best of what Islamic Spain stood for. Al-Andalus was a truly magnificent civilisation, part of a much bigger one that stretched from the Atlantic to Melaka, because it was open to the best and therefore was capable of producing among the world's best.

From the viewpoint of modern liberalism, al-Andalus had its flaws, but it was the glorious civilisation that it was because an essential spirit of tolerance and a remarkable intellectual openness nourished it. Muslims (Arab, Berber and Spanish), Christians and

---

[1] Refer to page 104.
[2] Refer to page 104.

Jews lived amicably together, all contributing to the greatness of al-Andalus. Although conscious of its Islamic identity, that consciousness was positive and open to all the possibilities of life, The sacred and the profane, the worldly and the non-worldly, the religious and the secular, were held in near-perfect balance. The distinguished scholar of Islamic civilisation W. Montgomery Watt makes a point in his history of Islamic Spain that resurgent Muslims of today should take note. Watt says although the idea of *jihad* (holy war) was used from time to time to swell the ranks of the army for a particular purpose, for the most part the running of the state was essentially based on secular ideas of governmental practice. Theoretical Islamic norms were always there in the background, and manifested themselves in practice in certain appropriate areas, but generally court life and administration were essentially quite pragmatic. It was this flexibility apparently that made it possible for the flowering of talents in all the major areas of the arts. Everyone knows of the Alhambra, the great Mosque of Cordova and other architectural splendours, but not many I think are familiar with the remarkable achievements of al-Andalus in the fields of learning and literature. The greatest names in these related fields are undoubtably Ibn Rushd and Ibn Arabi, both of whom were pretty unorthodox and universalist in spirit. Ibn Rushd, philosopher and physician, was, among his other notable achievements, responsible for the survival of Aristotle's *Poetics*; he saved that "wonderful fruit of pagan civilisation" (the words are Naguib Mahfouz's, Islam's first Nobel laureate) - saved it from oblivion in his commentary on the Greek philosopher. In Islamic philosophy, one of his most famous works is *Tahafut al-Tahafut* (The Incoherence of Incoherence) in which he defended the place of philosophy in religion against the assault on it by that highly influential orthodox Persian theologian Al-Ghazali in his book, *Tahafut al-Fasafah* (The Incoherence of Philosophy). Ibn Arabi is to me one of the greatest mystic thinkers and poets the world has produced. The universalism of his vision is epitomised in those words of his which I quoted in one of my columns: "In praising that which he believes, the believer praises his own soul; it is because of that that he condemns other beliefs than his own. If he were just, he would not do it; only he who is fixed on a certain particular adoration is necessarily ignorant of the intrinsic truth of other beliefs" (*Fusus al-Hikam*, or The Bezels of Wisdom). He reinforced those marvellous words with an even more marvellous quotation from a fellow Sufi, Al-Junayd: "The colour of water is the colour of its receptacle."

The achievements of al-Andalus in poetry are quite impressive too, though I don't think it produced any poet of the status of Abu Nuwas of Baghdad, or Hafiz of Persia. The poetry of al-Andalus is distinguished by its sense of *la dolce vita* (the sweet life), a hedonism that is by no means unIslamic. Love, of course, and the sense of the impermanence of life and pleasures are the recurring themes of the poetry. Here's a short sample: "A twisting curl/ Hung down, to hurl/ My heart of bliss/ To the abyss./ The sable tress/ Of faithlessness/ Lent deadly grace/ To faith's white face./ My heart doth fly/ Assaulted by/ The mallet of Your tress, my love,/ As white as day." (*Al-Husri*, 'The Tress', translated by A. J. Arberry). Here's another one, called *Poet's Pride*, by Ibn Ammar: "I am Ben Ammar: my repute/ Is not obscure to anyone/ Except the fool, who would dispute/ The splendour of the moon and sun./ It is no wonder if I come/ So late, when time is at an end:/ The glosses that expound the tome/ Are ever on the margins penned." (Translated by Arberry).

One of the remarkable things about the poetry scene in al-Andalus is the number of women among the poets; the names of more than 30 are recorded in Arab chronicles. There was an unusually high rate of literacy among women of all classes then, especially in Cordova when the Umayyad Dynasty was at its heights. One of these poets is Habsa Bint Al-Hajj Ar-Rakuntyya (1135-91). Here's one of the surviving poems of Habsah, a piece distinguished by its earthy wit, which she wrote jointly with her lover, each writing alternate lines. The poor man referred to in the poem was a fellow poet who kept interrupting the lovers at their secret meeting in a garden with distracting messages, until he was stopped by an unfortunate accident, a fall into a cesspit: "We have been freed from that poet/ By someone falling in the shit:/ Go back to your pit, son of shit,/ No matter who might have made it/ ... You fuddyduddy, shit-lover, amber-hater,/ May God prevent you from having visitors/ Until they come to bury you." (Translated by Christopher Middleton)

Lorca, the infidel poet who claimed al-Andalus as part of his spiritual heritage, was appropriately buried by his fascist murderers near a spring not far from Granada, called Fuente Grande (Big Fountain). The Arab name for the beautiful and much-loved spring was Ainadamar, 'The Fountain of Tears'. One of the Muslim poets had left a record of his feelings about Ainadamar. "Is it my separation from Ainadamar," he wrote, "stopping the pulsation of my blood, which has dried up the flow of tears from the well of my eyes? Beside it the birds sing melodies comparable to those of Mausili (famous Arab musician), reminding me of the now distant past into which I entered my youth, and the moons of the place (in plain words, the local women), beautiful as Joseph, would make every Muslim abandon his faith for that of love."

Fugitive Thoughts on May 13

[15th May 1991]

The name of my son, Adam Kabir seems to intrigue people. Adam's O.K., but Kabir? After that Kabir? Which Kabir? Ala, that Hindustani film star-lah! Who else? There's no point getting annoyed with that (I happen to dislike the film star in question). I can't expect many people to know of that other Kabir, the legendary 15th Century poet-mystic of Benares. Even an established contemporary poet cannot compete with a film star; what hope has a poet who lived hundreds of years ago? Adam Kabir was born four years ago on May 13. The date of his birth had something to do with the choice of his name. No, Kabir the poet was not born on May 13; nobody, in fact, knows when exactly he was born. It's what Kabir stood for that was behind my choice of the name for my son. And what he stood for is precious to people who cannot forget the tragedy of May 13 (May 13, 1969 - the date of the bloodiest racial riots in Malaysian history.).

Just as the name Adam transcends the barriers of language, race, culture, and religion, the voice of Kabir, melodious and resonant across the centuries, affirms the oneness of man and of God. Kabir is revered by the mystics of Islam (especially the Islam of the Indian subcontinent), Hinduism, and Sikhism. Many legends are associated with him; but the most famous and also the most apposite to my present theme is the one about his death. After the poet's death, so goes the beautiful legend, his followers from among the Muslims and the Hindus quarrelled over his dead body. The Muslims wanted to bury it, the Hindus to cremate. Suddenly, the spirit of Kabir appeared and said: "Why are you quarrelling over a mere corpse? Stop it! Lift up the shroud covering the corpse. See what's under it." They did so and found masses of flowers. "Divide them among yourselves," said the spirit, and they did. (In a cynical version of this legend there is a grimly funny twist at the end: The Muslims took the flowers and buried them, the Hindus burnt them.)

I allude to his legend (the non-cynical version) in a poem I wrote in honour of dancer Ramli Ibrahim, who in this country embodies the triumphant spirit of art transcending the boundaries of race and religion:

> And like the spirit
> Of that impious Sufi,
> caught between the dark pit
> and the blinding fire,
> make your supple body sing,
> let it be
> the sunlit, infinite
> song of flowers.
>
> On this *layla* of *lila*
> there is no joy but Joy,
> there is no god but God.

Kabir in Arabic means great. That Kabir was a great soul whose vision of God and man as expressed in ecstatic poems we would do well to listen to, I have no doubt. Whether Kabir was a great poet I cannot judge, because he wrote in Hindi and his poems are mostly lyrics. The lyric is of all poetic forms the hardest to translate into another language; it's even more difficult when the lyric is mystical, as Kabir's are. Nobel laureate Rabindranath Tagore brought out a translation of Kabir in 1915. The selection, *One Hundred Poems of Kabir*, has been reprinted many times. Most of the translations are merely passable as poetry, but as an introduction to Kabir, the selection is useful. There have been several other versions since Tagore's. One of them is by the distinguished American poet Robert Bly whose *The Kabir Book* (1977) - consisting of extremely free renderings in contemporary American English of 44 poems, a few of which read better as poetry than Tagore's - offers an interesting contrast to the latter. Neither Bly nor Tagore worked from the Hindi original; Tagore translated from Bengali, Bly simply reworked the Tagore versions. Those who want to go deeper into the world of Kabir may turn to a comprehensive collection-cum-study by V. K. Sethi, *Kabir: The Weaver of God's Name* (Radha Soami, Punjab, India,

1984). The title of Sethi's book refers to both the literal and symbolic facts of Kabir's life and work. The poet was a weaver by trade and in his songs, he was an ecstatic "weaver of God's name". It seems that between the two vocations, the latter claimed his attention more.

There are many more legends than hard historical facts about Kabir's life. But scholars seem to be more or less agreed that he was the son of a Muslim weaver of Benares, that he didn't practice his trade very much, that as a weaver of ecstatic verses vibrating with devotion and love for the Divine, he was highly eclectic. The orthodox from among the Muslims and the Hindus were shocked by his allegedly blasphemous indifference to divisive religious categories. And his insistence on the truths of personal experience as opposed to the untested abstractions of theology was considered a threat. But what Kabir says is said by the great mystics of all religions, proving that in mysticism, all religions meet and affirm Oneness and Unity. "O, servant, where dost thou seek Me?/ Lo! I am beside thee./ I am neither in the temple nor in the mosque:/ I am neither in Kaaba nor in Kailash (abode of Siva) ... nor in Yoga and renunciation ... " (Tagore's translation). He even dared to say: "The Purana and the Koran are mere words;/ lifting up the curtain, I have seen,/ Kabir gives utterance to the words of experience ... " (Tagore). If all this sounds offensive to the fundamentalist Muslim, whose literal mind will no doubt take particular exception to that line about the Holy Book, listen to what the acknowledged Master of Islamic mysticism, Jalal-ud-din Rumi (d. 1273), says in his *Masnavi*: "The lamps are different, but the Light is the same:/ it comes from Beyond ... O thou art the kernal of Existence, the disagreement between Moslem, Zoroastrian and Jew depends on the standpoint" (Translation by R. A. Nicholson). Kabir's words about the futility of finding God or 'Truth' in either Yoga or renunciation was affirmed in his own life, for everything with him had to be tested by experience. He believed utterly in plain speaking about everything and he literally did what he believed to be right, flouting social and religious conventions with supreme indifference.

There are many tales about his persecution by both Hindus and Muslims. According to one tradition, a certain Sheikh Taqqi (variously referred to as Kabir's greatest Muslim foe, rival, or even disciple) came to see him one day, and found a pig tied up outside his door. The Sheikh, of course, rebuked him for keeping the unclean animal. Kabir replied, "I have an unclean animal outside my door; you have many unclean friends inside your heart: greed, envy, pride, anger and avarice." The same Sheikh Taqqi, according to another tradition, accused Kabir before the Emperor Sikandar Lodi of laying claims to Divine attibutes. The Emperor issued a summons for Kabir's arrest. Kabir took his time in responding. And when he was finally dragged before the Emperor, he just stood before him without saying a word. The Sheikh, who was regarded as a *pir* (saint) by his contemporaries, rebuked him, "Why do you not salute the Emperor, you *kafir*?" Kabir replied, "Those only are *pirs* who realise the pain of others, those who cannot are *kafirs*."

Kabir may have been hated and persecuted by the religious establishments, but he was popular with the masses. He composed his songs, mostly transmitted orally in his time, in a colloquial, idiomatic form of western Hindi. His followers today number about half a million, and his disciples, the Kabir Panthi, are the jealous custodians of his tomb. As usual with such highly individual spirits and reformers, a dreadful irony attended the subsequent fate of his name and memory. The man who poured scorn on all forms of idolatory has his image and book both worshipped by ignorant devotees. And that beautiful legend of the flowers shared by Muslims and Hindus - well, it remains just a beautiful legend mocked by fanatics who keep on spilling innocent blood in the name of God and religion.

Women, Perfume and Prayer

[16th September 1992]

I'm writing this on the morning of Wednesday, Sept 9. By the Muslim calendar, it's 12 Rabiulawal, 1413. It's a public holiday; right now thousands of Muslims are gathering on Merdeka Square after a procession from the National Mosque. Yes, it's the birthday of Prophet Muhammad (peace be upon him). While I'm tapping these keys, on the telly the Prime Minister is addressing the crowd on Merdeka Square. Banners among the crowd proclaim all kinds of pious aspirations. One of them announces the theme of this year's celebration: *Berjihad ke Arah Kecemerlangan* (Struggle Towards Excellence), though the word *jihad*, which in another context can mean holy war, may make 'infidels' feel a bit uneasy. The words of the Prime Minister, specifying the four qualities of the Prophet that Malaysians (including non-Muslims, I take it) must endeavour to emulate, are ringing in my ears as I tap the keys - keys to some understanding of the true significance of the Prophet to modern man. The four qualities are *sidiq* (truthfulness), *amanah* (trustworthiness), *tabliqh* (responsibility of conveying the truth), and *fatanah* (wisdom). Marvellous qualities, all; and necessary if our society is to achieve excellence in the moral and spiritual spheres, as well as those of politics and economic development. To the sceptic and the cynic, such words of idealism proclaimed on such an auspicious occasion smack of well-meaning birthday resolutions; ritualistically affirmed but not rigorously observed, much like those ubiquitous slogans that we are constantly bombarded with - you know, *Bersih Cekap Amanah* (Clean, Efficient, Trustworthy) and all that jazz. The Prophet as a revered model of being and behaviour is constantly affirmed, at least verbally, by all pious Muslims. Such an affirmation constitutes a conspicuous part of Muslim piety. Equally conspicuous but more deeply rooted in the heart is the extraordinary, if not unique, love for the person of the Prophet universally felt by Muslims. As Muhammad Iqbal, the poet-philosopher of Pakistan, strikingly puts it in one of his poems: "Love of the Prophet runs

113

like blood in the veins of his community." Like blood, yes. Note that and remember *The Satanic Verses*. This unusually profound love for the Prophet is, it seems, stronger among the Muslims of the Indian sub-continent than anywhere else. It has been said that to Pakistani and Indian Muslims, the figure of the Prophet is more sacred than even God Himself. With them, apparently, you might get away with insulting God but not the Beloved Prophet. Iqbal, in whose works the Prophet figures prominently as a model of the heroic self or 'superman', has a line in his poem *Javidnama* which most people would consider amazing in its assertion, but is apparently quite acceptable to a Pakistani or Indian Muslim. "You can deny God," says the line, "but you cannot deny the Prophet!"

This truly extraordinary regard for the person of the Prophet is something that Salman Rushdie, who hails from that part of the Muslim world himself, should have realised when he chose to display his satanic genius in the reckless way he did. If God has 99 beautiful names or attributes (the *al-asma al-husna*), the Prophet has even more. Each Muslim, depending on his imaginative capacity (or peculiarity), may treasure one particular name representing one aspect of the Beloved Prophet more than others, just as he may treasure one particular hadith more than any other. The name or attribute of the Prophet that I myself feel I have a special something for is *Kamil* (Perfect), and pretty close to it, *Munir* (Radiant). To the Sufis, especially those influenced by the theosophy of the great 12th Century Spanish-Arab mystic Ibn'Arabi, Prophet Muhammad is the archetype of the Perfect Man (*al-Insan al-Kamil*). This is a difficult concept to truly understand, and if understood, to explain. Briefly and crudely put, the Perfect Man in Ibn'Arabi's sense of the phrase is that man in whom the purposiveness of creation is consummated, who is the isthmus (*barzakh*) between the two poles of Reality: the link between Heaven and Earth, the invisible and visible. Talking of the visible/invisible immediately reminds me of the strikingly suggestive ambiguity of the Arabic word for invisible - *ghaib*. This word, according to Malise Ruthven (*Islam in the World*), can, depending on the context, "apply to a reality outside human sense-perception, or to the private parts of a woman - 'that which is (i.e. ought to be) concealed'." (I'll have to come back to this later.) The Perfect Man, says Ibn'Arabi, is at once "the eye by which the divine subject sees Himself and the perfectly polished mirror that perfectly reflects the divine light" (*Fusus al-Hikam* or *The Bezels of Wisdom*, translated by R. W. G. Austin). Mystical crap, did you say? Meditate on the word *ghaib*, and you'll, *insya-Allah* (God-willing), be granted a glimpse of the seductive heart of the mystery. Thinking of the Prophet as *al-Insan al-Kamil* leads me naturally to recalling my favourite hadith: "Women and perfume have been made dear to me, and coolness hath been brought to mine eyes in the prayer." (This is the best translation of the hadith I know; it's by Martin Lings, the author of the best modern biography of the Prophet, who informs us that "coolness of the eyes" is a proverbial Arabic expression signifying intense pleasure.) This beautiful hadith also happens to be the one which Ibn'Arabi chose to meditate on in his chapter on Muhammad in *Fusus al-Hikam*.

On the birthday of the Beloved Prophet, while my fellow Muslims on Merdeka Square are entranced by the Prime Minister's speech on the theme of *Berjihad ke Arah Kecemerlangan*, I'm mysteriously moved to quietly meditate on that most poetic of hadiths. Women, perfume, prayer ... Ibn'Arabi's interpretation of this hadith is not exactly easy reading, or easy to explain in the limited space given to me. So I'll simply quote parts of the suggestive summary by the English translator of *Fusus al-Hikam*. The 'perfume hadith', says Austin, illustrates "the underlying theme of triplicity in singularity ... This triplicity in singularity is ...the two fundamental poles of the God-Cosmos polarity, the third factor of the relationship between the two, all three elements (i.e. women, perfume and prayer) being united in the Oneness of Being." The first element of the triplicity, women, "represents the various aspects and nature of the cosmic pole, suggesting as it does multiplicity, nature, form, body, receptivity, fecundity, becoming, beauty, fascination ... " The Perfect Man may have "total involvement in the complex and multiple demand of cosmic life, symbolised by absorption in sexual union", but he'll take care to "correct" that total involvement "by the purification of remembering and reintegration into the world of the Spirit, symbolised by the major ablution after such union". This should explain what Ibn'Arabi means when he says that a man "may most perfectly contemplate God in woman." (Some feminists would probably dismiss all this as patriarchal crap; others might like the priviledged status of women it implies.) Austin's summary goes on to say that, according to Ibn'Arabi's view of things, "the attracting beauty of woman far from being a snare to delude man, should rather become for him that perfect reflection ... of his own spiritual truth, being, as she is, that quintessential sign or clue ... from which he might best learn to know his own true self, which is, in turn, to know his Lord". (Sorry for the convoluted sentence, but there you are.) It seems, if I may hazard an obvious gloss, the Sufis claim that to know yourself is to know God can best be realised through a woman. In other words, union with the *Ghaib* could best be realised through the *ghaib*. The second element in the triplicity, perfume, is a sort of connecting factor, "not entirely physical nor yet entirely spiritual". It "symbolises at once both the current of the creative Mercy and also the spiritual nostalgia that draws the human spirit back to its source in God". The last element, prayer, "symbolises the Spirit and its reflection in man"; its purpose is to make man fully aware of God. As with women, prayer has its own "perfume".

On the birthday of the Beloved Prophet, it is customary for Muslims to chant prayers and sing panegyric verses (*selawat, marhaban* and *qasidas*) in his honour, as well as listen to sermons. I prefer to express my reverence for and love of our 'Perfumed Prophet' by remembering in the very flow of my blood the perfection of his being; a perfection that embraces the human (very human) and the superhuman, the earthly and the transcendent, the creaturely sensual and the divinely spiritual, the visible and the invisible. And with that remembrance also to recall that the essential thrust of Islam, "the least 'other-worldly' of the great religious systems" (Malise Ruthven), is, *pace* the cheerless mullahs and puritanical fundamentalists, truly and marvellously life-affirming.

In Praise of a 'Wild Beast'

[17 May 1991]

Two Sundays ago, April 28, at about 3pm, I had a 'visitation'. Sort of. It was one of those boring suburban Sunday afternoons, and oppressively hot. After a heavy rice lunch, I felt like having a good siesta, which I often do, in the good old tradition of my lazy ancestors. But the noise of the telly from my next-door neighbour (probably a repeat of some excruciatingly silly *Drama Swasta* (TV Drama)) was unusually loud; it was impossible to sleep. The heat, the boredom, and the damned silly telly - it was enough to drive you mad. In fact, for a split second, I almost felt the onset of vertigo. I had a flash of a vision, of myself leaping across the room like a tiger, snatching the ancestral *kris* gathering dust in the corner of my study, storming into the street and running amok. I didn't do it. The threatening vertigo mercifully passed. I covered my ears with a pillow, and tried to retreat into my own world. Then a line or two of a poem by a long-dead Indonesian poet unsurprisingly came to mind: "*Aku ini binatang jalang/ Dari kumpulannya terbuang ...*" (I am a wild beast/ Driven from the herd ...) I thought of a poem of mine, written at one sitting a few years ago, on a Sunday afternoon exactly like April 28, a poem with the same title as the Indonesian one (*Aku* ('me')), its opening and closing lines in fact parodying those of that poem.

My *Aku* was actually an 'updating' of the other *Aku*. If the Indonesian *Aku* (written in 1943) was the defiant cry of the individual spirit, its sheer refusal to conform, my *Aku* is just the opposite. It's the *aku* of the era of the NEP - a good pious, patriotic Bumigeois who sits in front of the idiot box every Sunday afternoon, and every evening, his mouth gaping wide, a box of KFC in his lap, drooling and finger-licking his existence away and dreaming of going on like that for another thousand years. (The closing lines of the Indonesian poem read: "*Dan aku akan lebih tidak peduli/ Aku mahu hidup seribu tahun lagi.*"(And I don't care a damn/ I want to live another thousand years.) Thinking of the two *Aku's*, I suddenly felt a *rindu* (nostalgia) for the long-dead poet. It

had been years since I last read his stuff. So I went into the study
and pulled out the yellowish disintegrating copy of the book that I
had been carrying around with me ever since my school days. With
the pillow still covering my ears I went through the poems again,
and flicked through the few pages on his life and times. It was then
that I noticed the date of his death. April 28, 1949. The coincidence wasn't quite earth-shaking, but it was, I felt, a bit uncanny.
Chairil Anwar, my much missed brother, was the coincidence a
sign of some kind? Yes, Chairil Anwar - that's the name of the
poet. Chairil Anwar. Lovely name. The best of lights. Chairil Anwar.

His poetry, believe it or not, used to be studied in our schools;
he has been translated into English (notably by the American Bur-
ton Raffel); and for a long time after his death, he was a figure of
legend. Yet I am sure there are many people in our country today
who have never heard of him, let alone read his poetry. Among
Malay *sasterawan* (writers), dilettantes and literary hangers-on,
the name Chairil Anwar is still spoken of in some awe. They can
recite lines and whole poems by Chairil - especially that notorious
Aku. But I doubt that what Chairil stood for, and what poems like
Aku are saying really means very much to these people. After more
than 40 years, the defiant absolute honesty of Chairil Anwar is still
a challenge. A lonely figure in the Forties, when his country
was fighting for its independence and the poet for his, he
remains without peer, or true spiritual descendant, in the history
of modern Malay-Indonesian literature. He was the first, and probably the only, true bohemian and rebel the Malay literary world
has produced. (Our own Latiff Mohidin is the nearest to a bohemian we have had; at least he was one until a few years ago, and in
a sense he still is, in spirit at least, despite what appearance might
suggest.) Being a 'bohemian', like a bourgeois, is more a state of
mind and spirit than that of your bank balance. The true bohemian
treasures his independence in every sense of the word. It's just an
unfortunate fact of life that this independence often means a poor
bank balance, or no balance at all. Chairil Anwar literally lived
from hand to mouth in the Jakarta (or Batavia) of the 1940s. He
was a familiar of prostitutes, on one occasion (so legend has it), he
had to sell his last shirt to pay for his *nasi bungkus* (cheap rice
dish); and he died of not one dreadful disease but four - tuberculo-

sis, typhus, cirrhosis of the liver, and of course, syphilis. He was only 27.

I think it is at least arguable that the health and vitality of a nation's literature can be gauged by the existence or otherwise of non-conformists among its writers; non-conformists who may have to be sick in body, due to depravation, but alive in spirit. I am not of course suggesting that in order for our literature to be more alive and exciting than it is today, we have to have a few amoral bohemians who fornicate with total abandon in pursuit of that elusive poetic masterpiece, snatching what crumbs of rice he can on the way, dying of syphilis (or AIDS, as it would be today) with the bloodstained, pus-stinking manuscript of his final poem in his unrepentant hands. That bit about having to be sick in body for the sake of being vital in spirit was, of course, just a manner of speaking. It's the willingness to suffer for the sake of fiercely-held values that matters; and the suffering doesn't have to mean being incarcerated in prison, or even literally starving in some stinking squatter hut. Willing to suffer and at the same time able to enjoy life, to affirm its essential worth despite all its contradictions, pains and frustrations. That, I believe, was what Chairil Anwar somehow managed to do. Here's one or two anecdotes that suggest the spirit of pure spontaneity that was Chairil Anwar. A contemporary remembers him perched precariously on the edge of an open car, and shouting the poems of Walt Whitman or Rilke into the wind and the polluted streets of Jakarta. Another remembers him hiring a whore and making love to her in a park, just to know what it was like to make love in public. Dreadful behaviour, but forgivable, I think, in a poet like Chairil - if he can get away with it. There was something recklessly noble, beautiful even, in his personality. As a poet and polemicist, his voice could be harsh and grating, but was also capable of incredible tenderness. Read the prose pieces addressed to Ida, as well as the poems on his relationship to women and to God.

On the subject of women and God, and death too, Chairil could be searingly honest. None of the sentimentality and predictable pieties with him. And the language and form, refreshingly revolutionary for its time, perfectly match the honesty of mind and heart. On the subject of the inscrutable God: "*Ku seru saja Dia/*

119

Sehingga datang juga/ Kami pun bermuka-muka ... Ini ruang/ Gelanggang kami berperang/ Binasa-membinasa/ Satu menista lain gila." (*Di Mesjid*). "I screamed at Him/ Until He came/ We stare at each other, face to face ... This/ Is the ring where we must fight/ Destroying each other/ One spitting insults, the other gone mad." (*At The Mosque*). The double meaning in "*bermuka-muka*", inevitably lost in translation, is characteristic of the fierce honesty of Chairil; the Malay phrase means both 'face to face' and 'pretending', or 'putting it on'. On the subject of women and love, have a look at *Kupu Malam dan Biniku* (*A Whore and My Wife*) and *Bercerai* (*Parting*). He wrote a second *Aku* which I believe not many people know of. "*Ku jauhi ahli agama serta lembing katanya/ Aku hidup/ Dalam hidup di mata tampak bergerak/ Dengan cacar melebar, barah bernanah/ Dan kadang satu senyum ku kucup-minum dalam dahaga.*" "I keep away from preachers and their holy words/ so unsparing, drunk on sins/ I live/ In the very eye of the day/ whirling at the centre/ the pox gaping, boils festering/ And now and then a smile blooms which I kiss/ From which, in my thirst, I drink."

Chairil Anwar, I claim you as my brother. May your spirit live another thousand years. And may you do something to inject some sign of life into this dreadful, deadening smugness and complacent conformity that is much of our literature today.

Homage to the Strong and Lonely

[29th January 1992]

Introducing K. Das' nostalgic account of his boyhood encounter with Pearl Buck's *The Good Earth* (Books Page, Jan 4), the editorial note asked the question: "How many of us remember the first book we read as we stood on the threshold of adulthood?" I remember mine, read 34 years ago, very vividly. The book was a minor work by one of the world's major writers. It struck me so deeply that 34 years later, I could recall it as if I had only read it yesterday. I can even remember the book as a distinct physical entity; the size, shape, colour of the cover (yellow and white with the title in black type), the name of the publisher (Heinemann), and I sometimes fancy I could still recall the special smell of the paper too. Before writing this piece, I got hold of a copy from the university library to check my memory against the text. Reading it again after so long, it was quite amazing how much I could anticipate, not so much the story (that was nothing) but the dialogue. And my memory these days isn't quite what it used to be. I can think of a number of reasons why the book had such an impact on me. I aquired the habit of reading very late - not until my late teens. Until then, I was totally uninterested in books. I was about 16 when I opened up the thing; and it proved to be the one that seduced me into becoming a lover of its kind for life. Why this particular book, and not others encountered at about the same time? The subject and theme of the book had a lot to do with it. It was what you might call an 'adult book', about adults and with an 'adult theme'. And I, being a late developer, encountered it at just the right time, when my mind was beginning, somewhat belatedly, to awaken. Unlike many compulsive readers, my first 'real book' wasn't *Alice in Wonderland*, Grimm or Andersen (all of which I only read for the first time as an adult, discovering them together with my children). My childhood was almost totally unblessed by the presence, the sight and smell of books. My father was an avid reader but of nothing other than newspapers; the only book in the house, other than school texts, was the Quran. I therefore had no childhood so far as reading was concerned. The first real book I read was also the first important book encountered as I stood "on the threshold of adulthood".

The book was a play by the 19th Century Norwegian playwright Henrik Ibsen. It's called *An Enemy of the People*. Compared to the plays by which Ibsen is best known to the world - *Ghosts, Hedda Gabler, The Wild Duck, The Master Builder, Peer Gynt* - *An Enemy of the People* is, considered strictly as a dramatic work, very minor. But to me, 34 years ago, it was a sheer masterpiece and thematically a real eye-opener. It was probably the first play I ever read; and I rather like the idea that the first book of my life should have been a play even though it wasn't one by Shakespeare. And I also rather like the idea that a play with such a ringingly ironic title, *An Enemy of the People*, should have had such an impact on my adolescent mind. Looking back from the vantage point of my half-century, and succumbing for a moment to the temptation of the pretentious, I wonder if there wasn't an element of 'provincial prophecy', and ironic too, in that teenage encounter between the 'Norwegian apostate', whose controversial plays like *Ghosts* drew the wrath of his countrymen on him, and the *kampung* boy from Malacca who at that age had only one conscious notion concerning the purpose of education - to obtain the passport to social success and thus become 'one of them'. *An Enemy of the People* (written in 1882, and first performed in Christiania the following year) is about a 'water crisis' not unlike the one my poor old Malacca had to suffer for so long only recently. The 'water crisis' in the play is the catalyst of the moral drama of integrity versus corruption, truth versus lies, courage versus cowardice, moral independence versus spineless conformity, the lone individual versus the compact majority. It tells the story of Doctor Thomas Stockmann, the medical officer at a small Norwegian spa, who discovers that the Baths, on which the prosperity of the town and the power of the ruling class depend, are contaminated. Being a man of integrity, charmingly full of faith in his fellow-men and naively stubborn in some ways, it is obvious to him what is to be done. To the Mayor, who happens to be his brother, what is obvious is something else entirely. He knows what making public the doctor's discovery would mean - to his position as Mayor who was responsible for the actual construction of the Baths and the way the pipes were laid, and to the prosperity of the town, especially of the middle class to which the Mayor belongs. The editor of *The People's Herald* and his printer are at first on the side of the doctor. But it is hinted fairly early in the play that their motives are dubious, as events subsequently prove. In the name of public opinion, they turn overnight from being the would-be champions of integrity and accountability to being the leaders of the pack that hounds the doctor. The play, in part inspired by two actual incidents, was written at a furious speed, without the usual lengthy period of gestation characteristic of Ibsen's writing habit. He was obviously in an uncompromising mood, the speed of the writing dictated by red-hot fury at and contempt for the mass mind; the mob hysteria in the Press that greeted the publication the previous year (1881) of *Ghosts*, a play essentially about servitude to meaningless conventions, must have haunted the writing of *An Enemy of the People*. The state of mind in which the play was written probably accounts for the relative crudity of its dramatic development, the use of some rather heavy-handed ironies (dramatic as well as verbal) and the simplistic characterisation of some of the secondary charcters. (Arthur Miller, when asked to do his own American version of the play in 1950, at a time when the freedom and integrity of the American theatre itself was under threat from the tyranny of the mob, felt compelled to rework the play to strengthen its dramatic texture.)

But, crude and simplistic though the Ibsen play may be in some ways, that very crudity is paradoxically part of its appeal; it has the rawness and immediacy of passionate commitment, of the thrill of taunting topicality, minimally mediated by the distancing refinement of art. Perhaps, innocent as I was of art on the fateful day 34 years ago, Ibsen spoke to my adolescent self with a directness that went straight to the liver (*hati*) of my mind.

I can still remember quite strongly the innocent thrill with which I thundered to the *kerbaus* (buffalos) in the *kampung sawah* (padi fields) Doctor Stockmann's passionate declaration of faith in spiritual elitism that concludes the play: "The strongest man in the world is the man who stands alone." (Miller's version of the line is much better: "You are fighting for the truth, and that's why you are alone. And that makes you strong - we are the strongest people in the world ... *(Crowd noises build)* And the strong must learn to be lonely.") I thundered the line to the *kerbaus* as if it was a revelation just granted me, quite unaware of its implications in the actual world. Perhaps that was the moment when my mind became contaminated by the foreign virus of arrogance and plain speaking. I was naive then, and my naivety perfectly answered to Stockmann's own brand of naivety, one that moved from the populist, with its faith in the "compact majority" and the so-called "progressive and independent Press", to its opposite: an elitist arrogance or *hubris*, an utter contempt for the forever changeable mass mind and the equally changeable "liberal Press". (*An Enemy of the People* really makes the words 'liberal' and 'progressive' sound quite obscene.)

But naive though Doctor Stockmann is at the beginning of the play, and disturbingly elitist he may perhaps be at the end, he remains essentially a character the intelligent and sensitive reader can empathise with. He dominates the play with the sheer energy of his passion - naivety, arrogance and all. And it is worth noting that, unlike many fighters for a cause, Stockmann isn't shy of what his puritanical brother would call "hedonism" and "self-indulgence"; he loves good food and drink, and loves to see others enjoying themselves. In some ways, Stockmann is Ibsen himself, one of the world's most uncompromising playwrights. It is no wonder that the role is the favourite of Stanislavsky, widely acknowledged as one of the world's greatest actor-directors.

Jebat, Gomez and Certain Feudal Matters

[16th December 1992]

During the Malay Literature Week held in London in September 1992, Usman Awang's play *Matinya Seorang Pahlawan* (Death Of A Warrior), about the amok-rebellion of the notorious Hang Jebat (a celebrated amok-rebel in traditional Malay literature, who defied his sultan for unjustly condemning his brother warrior, Hang Tuah, to death), was staged. The production was in the original language, but an English translation of the play, published on the occasion of the Literary Week, was made available for the non-Malay-speaking audience. Those Englishmen who happened to have blundered into the theatre where Jebat's amok-rebellion was staged, and got a copy of the English version of the play, must have recently wondered about the Malay mind. By "recently" I mean in the wake of the news about Gomez and the Sultan of Johor which I hear was splashed in all the major papers in Britain. I hope the British Press also reported that Douglas Gomez didn't take the alleged royal assault lying down; that the man who had the guts to speak up about the fate of hockey in Johor, for which he was allegedly assaulted by His Royal Highness, also had the guts to go to a police station and do what any self-respecting citizen of a democratic State would or should do. I hope the British Press noted that not all Malaysians are wimps. By lodging a police report against someone hitherto thought untouchable, Gomez has made history. Never mind that the poor fellow, his face all badly bruised, had to wait for signals from the right quarters before he dared to lodge the report; the fact that the report was lodged is the significant thing. And don't forget that by doing so, Gomez most probably put himself and his family in danger. A taboo has been broken, and hopefully this historic moment will lead to the removal of the last vestiges of feudalism that still cling to our political system. From the way all the newspapers have been going on and the things that some leading Ministers have been saying about the Gomez affair, you would think a 'revolution', a mental one at least, had taken place. The floodgates to long-

125

suppressed sentiments have certainly been opened. I wouldn't be surprised if there are many members of the *rakyat* (people), of all races and faiths, who feel secretly envious of Gomez and the royal treatment he was alleged to have experienced at Istana Bukit Serene (The Sultan's palace). It's not often that one has the chance to lodge a police report that will go down in history. If you can't be a Hang Jebat, a Hang Gomez will do. Who knows, a thousand little Gomezes might just one day make a mighty Jebat.

I think the time is right for us to talk about old Jebat again. Jebat as the archetypal rebel in Malay literature and the changing perceptions of him in the imagination of the Malays - that will be the theme of my sermon today. For a long time Hang Jebat was a much-maligned name. In the feudal mind of the Malays he was the epitome of treason and violence. The text which gave rise to this negative image of Jebat is the classical romance *Hikayat Hang Tuah* (probably written in the 16th or 17th Century). In one form or another the *Hikayat* must have been a favourite text for recital both in courts and *kampungs* (villages), for the reading aloud of *Hikayats* was very much a feature of the essentially oral culture of the ancient Malays. Thus the negative image of Hang Jebat was imprinted for generations on the minds of the Malays. In the Sixties there emerged a number of writers with more or less liberated consciousness who were impelled to reinterpret or rewrite the myth of Hang Jebat and turn the wild warrior into a rebel hero. I say "myth" because the figure of Jebat from the *Hikayat* had over the centuries acquired the status and resonance of a myth. But the Jebat of *Hikayat Hang Tuah* is based on what is generally believed to be a historical person. Jebat is one of the five famous warriors of Malacca in the part-historical, part-legendary classic *Sejarah Melayu* (Malay Annals). But the curious thing about this account of the five 'Hangs' (Kasturi, Lekir and Lekiu, apart from Tuah and Jebat) is that it wasn't Jebat who committed the act of amok or 'treason'; it was Hang Kasturi. There have been a number of theories to explain the discrepancy: one of them suggests that Kasturi and Jebat were originally the same person who later got his identity split into two. Quite an intriguing speculation, that; I suppose the Malays can use it to claim that some unknown

Malay genius anticipated Sigmund Freud's theory of the split ego by a few centuries.

I'm more intrigued by the fact that both the names of Jebat and Kasturi have to do with smell: *jebat* (from Persian and Arabic *zabad* or *zubad*) means the strong musky perfume known as civet - thus *musang jebat*, the civet cat; *kasturi* or *kesturi* (the sour lime; *citrus acida*), *bunga kesturi* (the scorpian orchid), and also *musang kesturi* (civet cat, again). *Musang jebat* and *musang kesturi* - same animal; that should support the idea that Jebat and Kasturi were originally one person. I find the musky odour linking Jebat and Kasturi intriguing; musk is universally associated with passion and sexuality because of its reputed power as an aphrodisiac. It's also interesting that the names of the two warriors are linked to the same animal, one with a powerfully distinct smell. The idea of a powerful smell suggested by his name reminds me of Jebat's resounding line from *Hikayat Hang Tuah* about his name becoming famous through the ages because of his act of defiance against the Sultan. In other words, the odour of the blood, sacrificial blood if you like, spilled by Jebat would haunt the Malay mind for generations. The odourous name of Jebat also reminds me of my favourite scene in *HHT* (*Hikayat Hang Tuah*): of Jebat reciting a *hikayat*, his voice so bewitching that the Sultan falls asleep in his lap and the maids of the palace literally lust after him. I have always thought that the Jebat of *HHT* is more of a hedonist-anarchist than a purposeful political rebel. I disagree with Kassim Ahmad's 1960's reading of this Jebat as a rebel against the feudal order, a prophet of modern Malay nationalism, even a democrat of sorts. I think the then-leftist Kassim's interpretation is a case of ideological wishful thinking which does violence to the text. Although it's true that the immediate motive for Jebat's amok is revenge for the unjustly condemned Tuah, and that the alleged act of 'treason' is the defiance of an unjust and irrational sultan, it can only be called a rebellion in a limited sense. And that sense doesn't quite include the political in the strict meaning of that word. Jebat's act is a highly individual gesture in the name of friendship, not of the oppressed *rakyat*. How could it be in the name of the *rakyat* when hundreds of innocent people (bystanders and the women of the palace) are butchered by him in his amok frenzy? And he is boastful of his butchery, too, confident that it will make his name infamous for generations to come. Although Usman Awang's play also makes Jebat a rebel hero, a martyr for justice (*keadilan*), his is a legitimate refashioning of the myth of Jebat. Legitimate because it is a play, a work of creative imagination, not an academic thesis which Kassim's little book is. But even Usman's Jebat is in one basic way not very different from that of *HHT*. Although in his simple but tightly constructed play he focuses on Jebat as a sort of political rebel, and he makes his hero truly human and humane (for example in his relation with the Sultan's favourite concubine, Dang Wangi, who he has made his own), Usman's Jebat still echoes a crucial line of the original Jebat, a line that boasts of his butchery and determination to take as many innocent lives as he can with him. The *hikayat* Jebat says: "*Sepala-pala jahat jangan kepalang; kuperbuat sungguh-sungguh.*" (If I am really to do evil, I won't do it half-heartedly.) Usman's Jebat says: "*Buat baik perpada-pada, kalau jahat, jahat sekali.*" (If you want to do good, don't overdo it, or do it within reason; if you want to do evil, do it thoroughly.) Usman's line is in fact a reversal of a well-known pantun: "*Orang daik memacu kuda/ Kuda dipacu deras sekali/ Buat baik berpada-pada/ Buat jahat jangan sekali.*" (The second couplet means: "Do good within reason/ And don't do any evil at all".)

But Kassim's ideologically slanted interpretation of *HHT* and Usman's recreation of the Jebat myth aside, it has to be said that the original Jebat of the *hikayat* is a figure of tremendous importance in the slow process of the mental liberation of the Malays. In other words Jebat's rare act of defiance was ultimately liberating. The blood he spilled was sacrificial blood. We have to realise that given the social and spiritual milieu of the old sultanate, in which the sultan was a demi-god whose *daulat* (a mysterious sacred kingly power) was so forbidding that any act of defiance, however mixed or ambiguous in motives and nature, was an event of immense importance. Defying the *daulat* is called *durhaka* (treason), a word with connotations as cripplingly powerful as *daulat*. The idea of *durhaka* was, and perhaps still is, so unthinkable to the Malay mind that Jebat, who was so consumed by *sakit hati* (brooding angry feelings, an amok symptom) because of the Sultan's unjust treatment of the loyal Tuah, was driven to run amok. Amok, yes! It's a much misunder-stood

128

phenomenon, amok is. Commonly seen as an insane motiveless frenzy, it in fact has, deep down, its own, peculiar rationality. Often a man runs amok (women don't; they *latah* instead) because of some perceived insult to his dignity and sense of manhood, or even the dignity of someone very dear to him. I imagine when the amok is in the grip of his *sakit hati*, of its brooding sinister stillness, all kinds of defiant images must be criss-crossing his tortured mind. Jebat in his *sakit hati* must have gone through something like that. And that Adam fellow too, perhaps. Remember Private Adam? The poor guy who ran amok with a rifle in Chow Kit Road a few years ago? Adam, yes! His name too has a mythic, archetypal resonance. Like Jebat.

Noordin Hassan: *Malaysian* Playwright

[6th April 1991]

Noordin Hassan, whose first and marvellous comedy *Peran* (mask or comic actor), was staged in Kuala Lumpur last month, is a playwright-director with a rare combination of virtues. After all the nasty things I've been saying in *AIP* about the tribe of bumigeois *sasterawans* and *senimans*, it actually makes me feel good to praise one of them. It is made easier by the fact that this "one of them" is in some ways not quite 'one of them'. Otherwise I doubt I would be so consumed by the urge to sing his praise. "His praise" here refers both to the person of the author as a human being and to his works. It is an axiom in modern literary criticism that there is no correlation between the quality of a work of art and the moral character or personality of the author. A selfish, petty-minded, ego-centric bastard can, if he or she has what it takes, somehow produce a marvellous poem, novel, or play. Even a bloody chauvinist or fanatic, believe it or not, is not necessarily incapable of producing what a humanist, if he is objective, would have to call a good work of art. It may be that the fanaticism or chauvinism in such cases has been kept out, and that work therefore appeals to you because of its strong formal or other qualities. It is also not uncommon that a writer can be guided in real life by values that contradict those cherished in his works. The word for this contradiction is hypocrisy. And the odd thing is that we, if we are capable of aesthetic objectivity, would have to admit that he or she is a good or even great writer though a lousy human being. For the sake of those marvellous poems, novels or plays, it is just as well that the vast majority of us don't have the dubious privilege of personally knowing their authors. Some of you may find this rather amazing. You want to know what I find *really* amazing? That a bore or an insufferable prig can produce an interesting story, a charming poem or a brilliant play. I have met writers whose work I like but whose company I find excruciatingly boring or a pain in the neck. It's as if when they write in the privacy of their room, some mysterious power or agency transforms them. How the muse can be so unpredictable in her distribution of favours beats me.

Given all this, how marvellous it is to meet and know a writer whose character and personality we like as much as his work, and whose behaviour in real life doesn't contradict the values affirmed in his writings. Such a person is Noordin Hassan. Noordin is the most courteous, the gentlest and the least pretentious of the *senimans* and *sasterawans* I've met. Neither his ego nor his head is swollen. He is also a uncommonly intelligent playwright-director with a highly individual style and a marvellous sense of theatre. His theatrical consciousness is multi-dimensional, capable of blending the traditional and the modern, and thus generating images and resonance that transcend barriers.

Noordin may be soft-spoken, but do not assume that the softness of his manner means a lack of moral or intellectual spine. Whoever thinks so should recall one of the most shameful episodes in the history of modern Malaysian theatre, and how Noordin, who rarely engages in polemics, reacted to it. The episode I mean is the blindly savage attack on Noordin by one of his fellow playwright-directors, Khalid Salleh, a man subject to sudden seizures of epileptic chauvinism. The attack, published in *Berita Harian* in 1986 after the staging of *Anak Tanjung*, was basically not unlike the attack by Mohd Affandi Hassan on Prof Muhammad Haji Salleh which I dealt with in this column about two months ago. Muhammad Haji Salleh was accused of being anti-Islam; Noordin was savaged for having allegedly sold out to the non-Malays. The article didn't deserve to be published even in a gutter newspaper. The tone was hysterical and the allegations meaningless and totally without foundation. What provoked it was apparently the positive treatment of Malay-Chinese relationships and the sympathetic portrayal of non-Bumi characters in the play. And the fact that Noordin has a Chinese wife must have helped to fuel the demagogic rhetoric of the critic even more. Noordin, whom I suspect doesn't get really angry easily, wrote a stinging reply. But the sting was lost on the thick skin and even thicker brain of the chauvinist.

Noordin knows what he believes in; and he is very much his own man. This is so even, especially when there is a coincidence of personal perception and that currently approved by his community or society of fellow Bumis. He has the mind and imagination as well as the faith, the sensibility and artistic discipline to embody his values and his vision in the form of a truly living theatre. His is among the few which come nearest to that difficult thing called 'Malaysian' rather than Malay theatre. Even when he is motivated by a deep-seated concern for the future of his race or inspired by the desire to dramatise what he perceives as compelling religious truths, the Malaysian spirit is never far from his heart and his art. Aspiring young dramatists should think of him and his kind of theatre as a model to emulate. With him, pride in his racial and cultural heritage doesn't lead to the mind being trapped in the divisive categories of race and religion. He is open to the sheer variety of life, just as he is open to the marvellous possibilities of the theatre. He takes his theatre very seriously but is never solemn about it. His delight in the sheer fun of theatre-making communicates itself to the audience seductively. And that urge to delight ensures that in his plays even serious matters can be treated with wit and humour without compromising their seriousness. The wit and humour of Noordin's plays have their roots in folk imagination enhanced by modern Western influence such as surrealism (most evident in his plays of the Seventies).

Since his first major play, *Bukan Lalang Ditiup Angin* (1970), Noordin has been a dramatist whose profound social concerns have always had a religious dimension. In the last decade or so, the religious dimension has become more pronounced, but never (with the possible exception of *1400*) at the expense of theatre. Being a 'natural' theatre man and an open-minded humanist despite (or because of?) his religious faith, Noordin seems to know instinctively that true religious concerns must embrace reality (both social and metaphysical) in all its complexity and variety. In his best plays, he doesn't preach; he shows, knowing full well that the language of theatre has a special kind of power and penetration. This was shown once again in his new play *Peran*, a hilarious satire on the theme of big heads and small heads, of swollen fantasy and painful reality. The comic form Noordin had chosen for this play dramatises even more suggestively and compellingly the ambiguous complexity of his vision of man and himself. Considering that Noordin had demonstrated his talent for visual and verbal satirical wit in his earlier plays, it is

132

rather surprising that he never attempted a comedy until *Peran*. When asked why he hadn't, he said that he was afraid of the temptation of frivolity that comedy as a form offers. That I thought was a rather funny reason. Now that *Peran* has been a great success both as entertainment and as a piece of serious theatre, I hope Noordin will write more comedies in future.

In Memoriam Isako San

[13th November 1991]

I can't claim to know him well personally, just enough to know
that his kind is rare and his death a sad loss. Dato' Ishak Haji
Muhammad, journalist and novelist, and nationalist oddball,
better known as Pak Sako. I remember well and quite fondly the
two novels on which his literary reputation rests, and also his
spicy and entertaining columns in *Utusan Malaysia* (a leading
Malay daily) and *Gila-Gila*. The man himself I'd met only two
or three times. The first time was about seven years ago, when
he came to Universiti Malaya, where I was then teaching. We met
in the famous Baccha's canteen in the Arts Faculty. I had long
wondered if the writer in person would be as interesting as his
writings and the rumours one heard about him. It is a pleasure to
report that the answer was yes. I was struck, though, by
something about him that the rumours concerning his political
and literary antics, both past and present, didn't quite lead me to
expect. He was soft-spoken and wasn't at all provocative in what
he was saying. Perhaps it was the academic environment that
made him seemingly reticent that day. But I was sure that the
reticence had an eloquence of its own; he was obviously
watching the academic scene and the pretensions of the puffed-
up little minds there. I certainly thought I saw a glint of impish
irony in his eyes. I was also struck by the smartness of his dress;
a fashionable bush jacket, no less. "Did they say he was a
'bohemian'"?, I murmured to myself; the 'rolling stone' who was
justifyably proud of the fact that he had not gathered any moss?
But that bush jacket which, I was told, he sometimes wore with
a stylish cravat, didn't quite mock his reputation as a plain-
speaking and plain-living champion of the common people. The
image of Pak Sako as a dashing frequenter of cabarets, and later
as the 'dandy' of Chow Kit Road and resident wit of the New
Hotel in Jalan Raja Muda was nutured by the same source as
that which fed his passion for life, and for the justice and
freedom without which that life would have been meaningless.

134

He always liked to keep in touch with the common people, but there was nothing about him that was even remotely like the self-conscious middle-class poseur compelled for ideological reasons to go slumming among the *rakyat*.

He may have been soft-spoken but his speech, like his writings, was often spiced with sharp and earthy wit, his famous humour salaciously sly, nicely vulgar, and his notorious scepticism of people and politicians always wryly ironic, quite often given an added punch by a fitting *pepatah* (maxim) or *pantun* (four-line Malay verse). He was a traditional Malay enough to be compulsively fond of the *pepatah* and the *pantun*. He even had a column called 'Pepatah Petitih' in the popular humour magazine *Gila-Gila*. These have been collected and were published in two volumes in 1989. The fact that Pak Sako was invited by *Gila-Gila*, a magazine aggressively committed to youth and hedonism, and that the old man enthusiastically accepted the invitation to be a *gila-gila* (literally 'mad-mad', i.e. eccentric) columnist speaks volumes for his natural talent for being at home in any generation, and to be a bridge between the old and the young. Many of his surviving comrades and proteges, like Pak Samad Ismail, consider him a 'typical Malay', but in the best generously open sense of that ambiguous phrase. As a good 'typical Malay', he was earth-bound, *kampung* (village)-rooted, but very far from being a Melayu with a *katak-bawah-tempurung* (frog under a coconut shell) mentality, either personally or ideologically. He was the type of Malay nationalist whose concern for his race was informed by a breadth and generosity of vision; his native intelligence and instinctive lust for life, if nothing else, made it easy for him to laugh at the rhetoric of chauvinism. He could number many non-Bumis among his friends and admirers: even Lim Kit Siang (the leading Chinese Opposition politician) became his champion in Parliament.

It was basic common sense and instinctive humanity in him, not abstract idealism, which made him stress the need for mutual tolerance, repect and concern among the races of this country. Typically, he would remind his fellow Malaysians of the obviousness of this need by making a light but highly suggestive joke about it or illustrating his point with a tellingly earthy and risible anecdote culled from his own rich experience of life. Like that marvellous story he told in a speech at the gathering held in his honour at Dewan Bahasa dan Pustaka in 1987. In 1948, so the story goes, he was in a small party of detainees being transported from Taiping to the police station in the then Campbell Road, Kuala Lumpur. There was somehow a shortage of handcuffs, and Pak Sako had to share one with a fellow detainee who happened to be a non-Malay. Well, you know what it would be like travelling long distance chained to another person; you would have no choice but to be together all the time and everywhere - including the intimate moments when the call of nature is simply irresistible. As a parable of man being bound together by common humanity despite the difference of race, I can't think of a better story than that; and only a Pak Sako could tell it the way he did that night at Dewan Bahasa.

Pak Sako, yes. My 10-year-old daughter said the name sounded like Ajinomoto when we read the news of his death last Friday; and how right she was. Sako, as fans of the old man should know, is from Isako, which is the way the name Ishak was made euphonically tolerable for the Japenese tongue. Isako later became Pak Sako, thanks to Ishak Haji Muhammad's journalist friends. The 'I' was dropped and substituted with 'Pak' - and that natural process of repossession of a name made alien by the tongue of a former enemy carried a small but suggestive symbolic significance. The softness and sense of familiarity of 'Pak' as normally spoken by the Malays, and its connotation of spontaneous respect and easy but concretely felt sense of solidarity, *kampung*-kind and rooted in the common earth - yes, it's rather nicely symbolic that out of 'Isako' came Pak Sako.

I've always thought that the best way to honour the memory of someone like Pak Sako is to re-read his books. The two novels, *Anak Mat Lela Gila* and *Putera Gunung Tahan*, certainly can bear re-reading after the lapse of a few years, if only to appreciate once again the satirical wit of Pak Sako, a wit which is quite rare in modern Malay literature. Yes, go back to his books - and stop dribbling about what a great man and writer he was. The chorus of inane praise that greeted the old man's death was typically and quite sickeningly Malay. Having failed to give the man adequate appreciation for his service to the nation when he was alive, we overcompensate by cheapening the words 'great' or 'giant' in calling him "a great writer" or "a literary giant". Pak Sako himself would have been utterly embarrassed by such chorus of *katak bawah tempurung*. I can imagine him, still disoriented by the darkness of darkness, turning in his new grave with embarrassment for the inanity of his people. I can imagine him saying to the two black angels with green eyes, Munkar and Nakir, sent to question him about matters of faith: "Listen to them up there! Calling me 'great writer', 'Literary giant' and what other nonsense! My people, they've infected my name with their own lack of proper modesty and sense of proportion. When I was among them, most of them could only bitch and be envious ... I wanted to teach them pride, proper pride and faith in themselves, with due sense of realism and proportion ... Now look at them! They make me feel I've miserably failed ..."

Patriarch as 'Literary Lecher'

[6th November 1991]

Going through some recent issues of the literary monthly *Dewan Sastera*, I was drawn to an article with a titillating title by the Patriarch of Modern Malay Fiction, Datuk Haji Shahnon Ahmad. Called *Seks dan Proses Kreatif Para Seniman* (Sex and the Artist's Creative Process), it pretends to be an exploration of the analogy between the act of writing and love-making. When a *Sasterawan Negara* (National Writer) who is also a tireless champion of 'Islamic literature' (whatever he means by that pious term) writes an article with such a titillating title, one can't wait to lap it up. Frankly, I was curious about what made him suddenly write on the theme. Though sex as a subject has seldom been far from Shahnon's fictional writings, he has never, as far as I know, made it a subject of his non-fictional cogitations. In recent years, only one subject seems to engage his pen when he is not writing fictions. That subject is religion, especially in its relation to literature. The Patriarch as a novelist and as a *mulla* at times reminds one a little of Dr Jekyll and Mr Hyde. The Jekyll in him loves to pontificate, in articles and seminar sermons, projecting a public image distinguished by religiosity; the Hyde cannot resist the lure of the prurient, inadvertently revealing the writer's hidden fascinations and unsuspected obsessions. In the *Dewan Sastera* piece, the analogy between writing and love-making promises much but delivers little. The analogy is rather limited in the first place and Shahnon, who is not the first writer to be struck by it, has too many intellectual hang-ups to transcend the limitations of his subject. In prose that is convoluted, almost a parody of the Shahnon fictional style in its tortuous attempt at verbal variations, and made worse by a mess of metaphors and clichés, our Patriarch merely labours the obvious. I can imagine him caressing his word-processor and groping for the analogy between *proses kreatif* (creative process) on paper and *proses kreatif* in bed, and getting nowhere. What we have in the *Dewan Sastera* piece are sterile ejaculations.

138

If our Patriarch would like to see how a writer with real imagination handles a comparable theme, I can recommend him a beautiful poem by the Patriarch of Australian poetry, A. D. Hope. The poem called *The Double Looking Glass*, uses the story of Susannah and the lustful Elders in the Apocrypha to explore and meditate on the association of creativity and sexuality and the relationship between the imagination and the natural world. It suggests the conditions under which the intercourse of lovers, like the intercourse of the imagination with the world, can be spiritually fruitful. But this kind of exploration can only be possible if the imagination is truly free. Free to explore the theme with faith in the wonder of our own humanness, to the point where the pull of the profane and the seduction of the sacred are mutually reinforcing, and the essential mystery of creativity is thereby affirmed. Love-making and fiction-making are both acts of intercourse which strive to be fruitful through some kind of creative struggle. Both involve style and technique. The possibility of devising new modes and styles, of playing new variations in this game of making, is limited in both cases, less so in fiction-making than in love-making. (Even the *Kama Sutra* has to acknowledge the fact that varieties of sexual congress are not limitless.) Our Patriarch recognises the need for experiments in both cases. But he takes care to stress that the experiments must be *sah*. *Sah* means authentic; but it can also mean legitimate. 'Legitimate' immediately suggests *halal* (permissible by religious law). It is not surprising that our Patriarch should want to impose a limit to what is permissible in writing. And, knowing him, the limit would apply to both form and content; there are modes of writing which are *haram* (forbidden) and there are subjects which are taboo. As in love-making so it is in fiction-making; there are religious rules and laws to be observed. So, if pre-marital and extra-marital intercourses are forbidden, so are their literary equivalents (whatever they are). 'Literary sodomy', 'fictional fellatio' and 'epic cunnilingus' are no doubt *haram*. What about positions? Strictly missionary, of course.

In the context of the Malay novel, our Patriarch is regarded as an 'experimenter'. His 'experiments' in the early novels were adaptations or imitations of Western fictional techniques and forms, such as stream of consciousness. In the best of those novels, these

139

techniques were used with some intelligence. Recently his new novel was published. The title? *Patriarch* (why not *Patriak*?). Any attempt to experiment here? The intention is there, I suppose, but the so-called 'experiment' in this novel is boring, and, to me, anything boring is *haram*, or should be. The style could only be called verbal masturbation, absurdly prodigal in its endless ejaculations. The old Shahnon style of rhetorical repetitions which served the early novels well has in *Patriarch* become self-parody. The mindless use of words of English origin in many places in this novel, like the meaningless verbal repetitions of which it is a part, is a form of linguistic-literary corruption and could be considered a literary vice, and therefore 'sin'. Here are a few mild and short but still hilarious examples: "Kebiasaan selalunya *bermonotoni; monotoni* melahirkan kebosanan ... "; "Segala-galanya menjadi hiruk-pikuk, berkecamuk dan *chaotic* ... "; "Dia mati begitu segera, begitu *spontan*".

Patriarch is about a corrupt leader whose nickname gives the book its title. His progressive political corruption is reflected in the growing animality of his sexual congress with his wife. (Strangely enough, he only has intercourse within wedlock; no extra-marital nonsense for a man who flouts all other moral and religious laws!) Without any plot or even story in the proper sense, the book is divided into five parts. Between the *Prolog* about a river that is supposed to symbolise the process of corruption, and the *Epilog* which is heavy with an apocalyptic vision of the entire people running amok and the whole country drowned in blood, we get the bulk of the novel. This is divided into three parts unbroken by chapters - *Sintesis* (Synthesis), *Tesis* (Thesis) and *Antitesis* (Antithesis). Why *Sintesis* first? Because the novel begins with or near the ending, of course. This reversal of the Hegelian dialectic, in fact even the use of the very terms, strikes me as mere pretentiousness. *Sintesis*, the longest section, begins with the Patriarch's death and takes the reader back to the days leading to the death. This is interwoven with the reactions of four different groups of disenchanted people across the country. The section is distinguished by pages and pages of turgid prose unrelieved by paragraphs. (Shahnon might as well have gone the whole hog by omitting all punctuations à la Joyce and thus commit the mortal sin of boring his readers to snoring sleep.) *Tesis* takes the reader

140

back to the early days when the Patriarch, then known as Jasadiah, was beginning to emerge as a potential leader full of promise about justice and clean government. Again, this is interwoven with the reactions of the four representative groups, this time full of hope in the new leader. *Antitesis* is nothing but a mere elaboration of *Sintesis*. The reversal of the dialectic thus turns out to be an unrelieved verbal orgy that really tests the reader's patience.

Somehow I feel that somewhere at the back of the author's mind, before he started writing, there was a promise of an interesting idea and the glimmer of an authentic form appropriate to it. But something must have gone wrong in the intercourse between the imagination of our Patriarch (i.e the author) and the subject of his novel. It is revealing that it apparently never occurred to him to show the corruption of the Patriach (the character, I mean) as reflected in his language. After all, the corruption of a politician is usually first manifested in the corruption of his language, as is the aesthetic and intellectual corruption of a writer is reflected in his language.

Kiss My Arse - In the Name of Common Humanity

[11 & 18 November 1992]

I had a dream last night. Most of my dreams are quite weird, but this one was weirder than any I've ever dreamt. I think it was inspired by something that happened at the United Malay National Organization (Umno) General Assembly last Friday. At this gathering, this 'Assembly' of the dominant party in the governing coalition, a Kelantan delegate, thoroughly disgusted with the dirty tactics (note "dirty") used by ambitious Umno desperadoes in their premature campaign for next year's party elections, told an old filthy joke that brought the house down. The joke is about the quarrel among the various parts of the body as to which one is really powerful and therefore should be the boss. The brain says it is and should be in control of the rest because ... Then the mouth, the nose and so on; each with its own irrefutable reason for making the claim. The anus, naturally, has the last say. It triumphantly declares that it is more powerful than any of the rest, including the brain: if one fine morning it decides to close up for good the body is finished, man. Kaput!

Related to such an august gathering as the Umno General Assembly, the joke was truly edifying; so edifying that it inspired my weird dream. I dreamt that I was invulnerable (*kebal* in Malay). Neither the *keris* nor the *parang* could penetrate my skin; even the notorious Kelantanese *kapak kecik* that flies in the night at the bidding of its frantic owner couldn't harm me. It seemed that I had finally attained (in the dream, that is) the much sought-after *ilmu kepala tahi*.[1] *Ilmu* what? *Kepala tahi*. *Kepala* what? *Tahi*. This is no ordinary *ilmu*, man; this is esoteric *ilmu*. But *tahi*? *Tahi*??? I think you're just being your usual vulgar self again ... Of course I'm being my 'vulgar' self. I'm always 'vulgar' - vulgar in more than one sense you know: not only 'coarse' or 'filthy' (your

---

[1] *Ilmu*: mythical knowledge or power
Kepala: head
Tahi: shit

meaning), but also 'common' as in 'common people' (i.e. ordinary people, unashamedly close to the earth, and revelling in it).

But back to the IKT (less offensive thus abbreviated?). I tell you it's not something I dreamt up, though its 'reality' and efficacy were confirmed for me only in my dream. IKT is a form of magic power which the Malays used to believe in; some in the remote *kampongs* (villages) probably still do. (No, you won't find it in Skeat's *Malay Magic*; it's apparently too vulgar even for that huge tome.) IKT can be acquired (so my uncle told me) by snatching the sausage-like T (it has to be a 'sausage'; watery stuff's no good) as it emerges out of somebody's anus. This might be done on a Thursday night (Friday night to the Malays). I won't strain your tolerance of the 'vulgar' by going into the lurid details of the messy business. It's sufficient to tell you that it must be done in a certain way, and that after you've acquired the precious substance you must wipe your whole body thoroughly with it, the wiping accompanied by the recital of certain mantras. Then you must avoid water for the next three days. If you observe all this, you'll be *kebal*. *Insyaallah*. (And please don't listen to envious cynics who say that you're *kebal* because nobody would come near you anyway.) With IKT, you don't need your brain anymore; or rather your brain has come down and joined forces with your anus. What you've got now is a sort-of 'thinking anus'. The unity of the body, of the highest and the lowest, the refined and the filthy, is now truly yours. Hang on to it for dear life. Now, what has all this stinking business to do with literature? Literature ... yes.

Well, the dream, the old joke dredged up at the Umno General Assembly, the mysteries of IKT - all this reminded me of a curious novel I read earlier this year. And with it, the thoughts I have been thinking about on and off for quite some time on the subject of the vulgar, the filthy, the taboo, the 'last frontier' of the body, physical-spiritual, sensual-mystical body, in both literature and folk imagination. The novel is by a Tongan anthropologist-writer Epeli Hau'fa and titled *Kisses in the Nederends* (Penguin, New Zealand). This comic satirical novel is literally and symbolically about an arsehole. As far as I know, Epeli Hau'fa is the first writer to devote a whole novel to *the* hole. And in a way it is a perfect illustration and proof of the anus' claim in the Umno General Assembly joke that it is the most powerful part of

143

the human body; it can abuse its power to become the most tyrannical dictator and capable of subjecting man to the worst humiliation imaginable. *Kisses* is a tall tale, one of the 'tallest' I've read. Written in a style that is clearly influenced by the grotesque realism of François Rabelais, it is about a Tongan who suffers from an uncurable 'pain in the arse', an ulcerous fistulated anus. The book opens with a bang, a stinking assault of farting, followed by a duet between the mouth (snoring) and the anus (farting), and the hero's waking up with an excruciating pain in his bottom. Then the rest of the book takes the hero on a mock-epic search for a cure, from the bizarre treatments of traditional medicine to an organ transplant in an ultra-modern New Zealand surgery. (Yes, the hero ends up with somebody else's anus, a white woman's down there.) This disgustingly hilarious Tongan tall tale ends happily with the cured hero triumphantly proclaiming a new religion of true brotherhood (and sisterhood) of man. Its slogan? "Kiss my arse!"

You need to have a strong stomach to read and enjoy this book to the end. My wife doesn't; after a few pages she threw the little Penguin out of the window in utter disgust. The writing of *Kisses* was actually inspired by the author's own experience; poor Mr Hau'fa actually suffered from a terrible pain in the arse much like his hero's, a sort of piles which the Tongans call *kahi* (*k* not *t*). True to the South Pacific philosophy that laughter is the best medicine, the novel proved to be the best therapy for the author, who suffered from a psychological malady even after the successful operation on his anus. But the novel is not only a therapy in the form of a tall tale; it's also an allegory that carries a serious social and spiritual message for the Tongans and other island peoples of the South Pacific, and by implication for modern man in general. *Kisses in the Nederends* is to me a triumphant demonstration of my belief that there are many varieties of vulgarity - from the childishly obsessive to the soberly purposeful. In the hands of a comic or satirical writer with a talent and a fundamentally weighty intention, the vulgar and the filthy can be redeemed by art in the cause of a vision. François Rabelias in his *Gargantua and Pantagruel*, Jonathan Swift in his *Gulliver's Travels* and James Joyce in his *Ulysses* and love letters to his Nora are among the world's greatest 'filthy writers' in this sense.

Epeli Hau'fa is part of a long tradition, and *Kisses* shows that he has the makings of a mini Swift of the South Seas. Swift is probably the most familiar of the three, thanks to his *Gulliver's Travels,* a book which every reasonably well read kid knows. Kids reading filthy stuff? Not quite, because the *Gulliver's Travels* that kids read has been cleansed of all mind-polluting filth. Children's editions of the classic work are either simplified (for young kids) or published (for older kids) without the third and fourth books: 'A Voyage to Laputa' and 'A Voyage to the Country of the Houyhahams'.

The third book, a sort of proto-science fiction, recounts Gulliver's experience on the flying island of Laputa where he visited the School of Political Projectors at the Academy of Lagado; there he meets weird professors or projectors who are distinguished by their ingenuities in the service of the state. They have, for example, developed a special technique for discovering plots and conspira-cies against the government. The technique involves examining the diet of all suspected persons; finding out "times of eating; upon which side they lay in bed; with which hand they wiped their posteriors"; then to take "strict view of their excrements, and from the colour, the odour, the taste, the consistence, the crudeness or maturity of digestion, form a judgement of their thoughts and designs". The whole business is based on the belief that "men are never so serious as when they are at stool", and because of that their stool can tell us all kinds of things; for example "if the ordure has a tincture of green" that means when the suspect was having his stool he was "straining to think of the best way of murdering the king, but quite different when he thought only of raising an insurrection or burning the metropoles".

The fourth book of *Gulliver's Travels,* the one generally considered the most important of the four, narrates Gulliver's encounter with the tribe of super-rational horses, the Houyhahams, and their opposites, the filthy Yahoos, whose resemblance to himself Gulliver tries to deny. He is so seduced by the Houyhahams, creatures which embody for him the ideal of civilised being, and so disgusted by the stinking Yahoos (who warmly welcome his arrival on the island by defecating on him from a tree), that he goes mad in the end; back home in England he tries to live with horses, behaves and neighs like one, spurning the company of his fellow human beings who are all Yahoos to him. There has been much debate among scholars and critics about the meaning of *Gulliver's Travels*, especially Book Four. The debate has to do with Swift's real attitude to the Houyhahams: does he share Gulliver's admiration for the cold blooded super-rational horses or doesn't he? Related to this is the question of Swift's scatology, what its very pronounced presence in his writing means when we try to determine his attitude to man and to human nature.

Distinguished modern writers Aldous Huxley and John Middleton Murry were apparently the first to confront the blatant fact of Swiftian scatology which earlier writers on Swift had ignored or pretended didn't really exist. Huxley especially recognised the central importance of the scatological theme in both *Gulliver's Travels* and three of his later poems ('The Lady's Dressing Room', 'Strephon and Chloe' and 'Cassinus and Peter'). But Huxley's and Murry's conclusion, that Swift's scatological "obsession" (in Murry's highly suggestive phrase, "excremental vision") reflects a fundamental neurosis in the writer, a neurosis that made him a misanthrope or hater of human nature - this conclusion, I believe, is based on a misreading of Swift. I am with the American writer Norman O. Brown here. Brown, whose breakthrough book *Life Against Death* (1959) first offered a balanced reading of Swift argues convincingly that Gulliver's misanthropy is his, not his creator's. Similarly, Cassinus, in the poem 'Cassinus and Peter', who "lost (his) wits" on discovering that "Caelia, Caelia, Caelia sh--", shouldn't be confused with Swift. (Swift did go mad in the end, but not because he couldn't stand the fact that women 'sh--', as critics like Murry seem to suggest.) Cassinus is obviously a projec-tion of the universal neurosis of civilised man who cannot accept and revel in the fact of nature that the body is a wondrous unity - of the higher and the lower, the spiritual and the bestial. Civilised man (or rather over-civilised man) is haunted by that reality of our human nature immortalised in the famous words of St Augustine: "*inter urinas et faeces nascimur*" (the seat of love is the foulest place in our body - implying that our most exalted, most spiritual aspirations are bound to our soiled flesh). Over-civilised man represses and sublimates his animality and that's why he is sick.

Epeli Hau'fa, is a mini Swift of the South Seas and is clearly a writer who affirms that wondrous unity. The phrase "mini Swift", though, may not be quite accurate, it can suggest something that is more Swiftian than 'Hau'fian'. Swift, that "tiger" of 18th Century English literature is a master of satiric comedy that is distinguished by its uncompromising fierceness; a fierceness that is not quite 'Hau'fian'. Hau'fa in *Kisses in the Nederends* is relaxed where Swift in *Gulliver's Travels* and the satirical poems is fierce and furious; Hau'fa's hearty comedy is more Rabelaisian, wild and rompy - and hilariously breezy. In an interview with the New Zealand literary magazine *Landfall*, Hau'fa says:"I am by nature playful, and playing with words, obscene or otherwise, is an aspect of that nature. But that is only one aspect of my use of dirty language. I used it also for other purposes. Firstly ... I resorted to it as a way of presenting the effect of physical agony (that unrelenting "pain in the arse", remember?) on Oilei's psyche (Oilei is the aptly named suffering hero of *Kisses*), and on his relationship with those around him. But most importantly, I used it as a most unlikely tool for a discourse on love, purity and harmony ... " A comic satirical novel with an ulcerous fistulated anus as the prime mover and focus of the narrative - that kind of novel is "a discourse on love, purity and harmony"? I'm happy to say, yes. Unlikely? Well, the author himself is fully aware that his use of "dirty language" is "a most unlikely tool" for such a discourse. He even knows that "it's never been done or even thought of before". But that's what makes it fun; it's a form of creative experiment that shows that Hau'fa the anthropologist is also a true writer. Hau'fa asks the question that Rabelais asked centuries ago: "Why should we continue to loathe references to our organs of procreation and elimination, and not to other organs?" Such questions have implications that go beyond mere body matters. As Hau'fa puts it they lead to "other questions about social and cultural institutions". As he worked on the novel, laughing as he furiously scribbled ("I could not but laugh as I wrote"), the fundamental seriousness of the theme became more and more crystallised in his mind.

The idea or ideal of bodily unity (and equality) came to suggest other forms of unity (and equality) - such as the social and political (thus the use of language with political connotations in Hau'fa's descriptions of the "rebellion" of the body's lower orders, the bowels and the anus). "I seriously said to myself," Hau'fa recalls in the interview, "that if we give our organs of procreation and elimination the same consideration that we give other parts of our bodies, we would eventually eradicate most of the obscene expressions in language and therefore in thought. That should go a long way towards helping us to be more loving and caring of each other ... Oilei's search for a cure for his physical ailment is also a quest for purifying himself of violence and obscenity in language. Having attained his goal he invites everyone to kiss his arse. It is a joyous statement of the end of hatred, and a declaration of love for all mankind. It sounds bizarre but I'm serious about it ... " Bizarre maybe, but I can't agree with Epeli Hau'fa more.

In the novel the character who helps to bring the light to Oilei is a guru and yogi named Babu. Babu is a wily character who can be both a clever entrepreneur and a prophet of spiritual and social liberation. Babu's mission is to convince the world that "the anus is good, beautiful, lovable and respectable". He declares that "It's time that the status of the repressed lower organs" (note "repressed" and "lower" in both its psychoanalytical/biological and political meanings) "is recognised". He pointedly adds: "We treat our heads with respect and call our leaders heads. We could, with equal felicity, call them anuses." Babu prescribes yoga exercises for his patient, designed to make him learn to respect his own anus so that it becomes truly part of him - and smells to his nose "as the fresh bud of spring". One begins by learning to love one's beautiful anus, kissing it, meditating on it, inhaling its spiritual as well as physical aroma. Then the next step is to learn to love the anuses of our brothers and sisters. Babu demonstrates the truth and power of his teaching by kissing Oilei's anus with love and respect. The guru declares: "If the President of the United States and the Soviet Union do likewise at their next summit (sic) meeting there will be no more threat of nuclear annihilation ... As in most things we must begin from the top down. When the top meets the bottom, there will be eternal peace. The real obscenity, the novel says, is not the so-called "dirty language", but man made horrors like nuclear war. To ban that sort of obscenity from the life of man altogether we must learn to "greet, love, laugh and dance with each other in the middle of our zones of taboo".

The Spectre of 'Corporate-Lit'

[7th July 1993]

As president of the National Writers' Association (Pena), Datuk Ahmad Sebi Abu Bakar has left a remarkable stamp on the Malay literary world. He became *Ketua Satu* (First President) of Pena early last year in an election which was unusual in many ways - not least of which was the conspicuous display of power in the campaigns for the election. This election businessman Ahmad Sebi signalled the entry in a crucial way of the corporate presence into the literary sector, an event enthusiastically welcomed by some, less by others. The latter are of course the incorrigible sceptics or cynics who cannot but see the marriage of the corporate sector with the literary as 'unholy'. In less than a year, the corporate commitment of Ahmad Sebi has made itself more than acceptable to *sasterawans* (writers). In November 1992, he organised an unusual seminar on 'The Role of Language in Nation Building' where most of the papers were given by people from the corporate world. Unlike the usual *sasterawan*-dominated seminars, this one wasn't lost in the fumes of endless chatter about the *maruah* (honour) of the race or nation. It dealt with the nitty-gritty, confronting the actual problems that still seem to check the widespread use of the National Language in the private sector. Ahmad Sebi's belief in the importance of the corporate service to the literary world was endorsed by Gapena which made its recent *Hari Sastera* (Literature Day) focus on the role of corporations in literary developments.

Sebi's latest corporate gesture is the establishment of a Writers' Academy in the name of Pena. With the Prime Minister as its patron, the Academy, which is sponsored by several media and corporate organisations, will provide courses in creative writing, journalism, electronic communications, public relations and advertising. An article in the brochure on Pena circulated among those who attended the launching of the Academy last Saturday makes an interesting point about the writers' association and the political establishment. There is now, says the article, better communication between government figures and writers' organisations like Pena; this is so because of the young leaders among them who understand better our national cultural and literary aspirations.

One of these young leaders is Finance Minister Datuk Seri Anwar Ibrahim who was invited to launch the Pena Academy. In his speech, Anwar stressed the vital importance of writers in making Malaysians acquire a positive attitude towards the objectives of Vision 2020. Anwar's words reminded me very much of what the Prime Minister said in relation to the idea of 'Malaysia Incorporated' a few years ago. In his speech when tabling the Mid-Term Review of the Fourth Malaysian Plan, Dr Mahathir urged Malaysians in every sphere to be "totally involved" in development and nation-building. The scenario for the future envisaged by Dr Mahathir is mind-boggling: a radically 're-structured' society fully exploiting its natural resources and planning for a population of 70 million to support the mass consumption industry. With this 'futuristic' scenario in mind, the Prime Minister delivered a stern warning to writers not to shirk their role in helping to realise the great national dream. He told writers and publishers to actively foster the spirit of development and "work ethics" by producing writing capable of inspiring the masses. They were instructed to curb the publication of works that look sceptically at the 'futuristic' vision of a highly developed "re-structured" society. Vision 2020 poses a comprehensive list of challenges which, if fully met, will make our society the envy of the world. Just look at the string of adjectives used to describe that future society: united and integrated; psychologically liberated; secure and self-confident; mature and democratic; progressive and innovative; prosperous and economically competitive; and robust and resilient. Marvellous, aren't they? But if you look closely at the features of this ideal society, you'll see that some of them are quite utopian because the chances of their being realised are not strongly supported by past experience or present realities and trends. There are also contradictions between the implications of one objective and those of another. Because of these contradictions, there is a possibility that an objective considered less convenient will be sacrificed in the interest of another considered more politically expedient.

A writer who wants to write about Malaysian society in the year 2020 must have thought deeply about the Vision. He must know history, be critically informed about present realities, and be able to imagine what the future is likely to be considering those realities. He must be clear about his own values and those that are likely to govern the society of the future. He must take care to preserve a critical distance from his subject so that he won't succumb to mindless optimism. He must resist any temptation to sacrifice artistic integrity for the sake of propaganda. Last but certainly not least, he must be able to write. Writers often tend to be sceptical when it comes to grandiose projections. They tend to distrust anything that smacks of utopia. They are too conscious of human frailty and the temptations of power to be seduced by futuristic dreams. If they feel compelled to write about such dreams, they are likely to do it in the form of a cautionary tale, warning us against the possible perversions of noble dreams or the sacrifice of humane and democratic values on the altar of material development. The call for utilitarian development-oriented writing should worry poets most. This is because poetry, of all the literary arts, is the least sympathetic to the simplistic rhetoric of politics and corporations. Poets tend to be more stubbornly inner-directed than their fellow writers in prose. When poets give their attention to public matters, they tend to do so in defence of private values, or on behalf of humanitarian ideas inconvenient to pragmatic politicians. Whether socially idealistic or simply private, poetry tends to be the most 'subversive' of the arts; it 'subverts' the life-denying pieties of realist politics that put a premium on GNP at the expense of the social, spiritual and aesthetic health of the individual, that pursue technological development at the expense of the natural environment.

These political pieties are especially dangerous when buttressed by the pieties of revivalist religion, which is the fashion today in many countries, including our own. One arm around the Mullah of Regress, the other around the Moloch of Progress - and together they march backwards and forwards down the pit of the Rising Yen. 'Look East' is the banner, 'Work Ethics' the slogan; the example of mighty Japan (where the suicide rate is high) has to be emulated at all costs. The Government and multi-national corporations, generous with banquets, literary jamborees and other things, seem to know how to silently 'incorporate' even the most critical of the country's writers and intellectuals. A singing group called Korporatasa has recently been disbanded in the interest of individuality. I wonder how strong is the individuality and integrity of our writers against the spectre of *Korporatsastera* or corporate-lit..

Malay Lays of Life, Love and Laughter

[22nd May 1991]

The other day I had an argument about the Malays with a friend. This friend is a Malay himself, but highly critical of the race. "Very repressed ... Puritanical ... Must be the religion ... Just look at their (sic) literature ... So barren of mere pleasure ... Hardly any celebration of the feast of the senses ... Not a single work noted for its sensuality, eroticism ... " This friend, a veritable hedonist and a rather noisy one too, is fairly well-informed about Western literature but hopelessly ignorant about his own. (That of course didn't prevent him from making confident judgements about it.) I asked him if he had read *Hikayat Hang Tuah*. Of course he hadn't; and even if he had tried I doubt he would have gotten very far (all that endless string of 'verbal punctuations' - *maka ini, maka itu,* periodically broken by *hatta* - would have put him off, if nothing else). I told him the *Hikayat* was in some ways a 'hedonistic' work. Think of all those near-orgiastic scenes of eating, singing, dancing and carousing - and all those damsels and concubines.

I also shared with him my 'deviant' image of the notorious rebel Hang Jebat. In contrast to Kassim Ahmad's elaborate revisionist reading of Jebat as a political rebel and protodemocrat, mine is simple - that Jebat was a hedonist and sensualist. To me it's so obvious from the text that it's amazing nobody, as far as I know, had thought of it before. One of the most erotic scenes in classical Malay literature is found in this *Hikayat*. This scene, just preceding the famous amok of Jebat, shows the doomed warrior reading a romance to the sultan who is sitting on the palace *bendul* (threshold; a significant detail, this). Jebat's voice is so wondrously sensuous and seductive that all the palace *dayangs* (court damsels) and *gundeks* (concubines) are so aroused that they crowd in a near-trance state around the door to get as near as possible to him. Jebat's reading is followed by singing, his voice becoming more enchanting, so enchanting that the sultan actually lays his head in the warrior's lap and falls to sensuous sleep. In the light of the blood bath about to come, there is an under-current of the sinister in the uncanny sensuality of this scene. Sensuality and violent death - the juxtaposition is suggestive.

"Hedonism in *Hikayat Hang Tuah*?" exclaimed my friend. "Really? But that's all in the remote past. If hedonism was ever an essential part of the Malay make-up, it no longer is. It's the religion ... "

Is it true? First, is it true that a form of hedonism was an essential part of the Malay nature and philosophy of life? Second, is it true that hedonism has become so suppressed over the centuries that it has become almost alien to the race? Third, is it true that Malay literature in general is shy of celebrating the senses, so barren of sheer sensuality, so lacking in erotic moments? I'll deal with the third question first and then hazard some suggestions by way of answering the other two.

I think it is undeniable that modern Malay literature is not notable for its achievements in the evocation of the raw pleasures of the senses - particularly the erotic experience. There have not been many attempts anyway, and of the few, the ones that could be considered memorable are less than the number of fingers of one hand. But if you move away from modern literature and venture into the imaginative world of older times, you will find some remarkable moments of unashamed sensuality and eroticism. Significantly enough, most of these are found in the *pantun*, the one truly native and very Malay of the poetic forms. The fact that it is an oral form and more expressive of the life of the common folk than that of the courts is also significant.

I want to begin by looking at a curious pair of *pantuns*. They are not erotic or even sensual, but they will prepare you for the erotic and sensual ones to come. These two *pantuns* are curious because they share a more or less common opening couplet but make a statement in the concluding couplet that radically contradicts each other. Such 'contradictions' are as a rule nothing remarkable; but in this case it reveals something pertinent to my theme. Here's the first one:

Asam kandis asam gelugur
Ketiga dengan asam remunia

Nyawa menangis di pintu kubur
Hendak pulang ke dalam dunia

With all those *asams* (sourish, bitter-sweet fruits), what a dish we have before us! (I could write a whole thesis on Malay hedonism as manifested in the attitude to food and the vulgar pleasures of the gut.) The first couplet is untranslatable; the taste is in the very sound of the words. The sound of the names of the various *asams* poetically ferments the fierce yearnings of the soul about to leave the earth and all its pleasures (the Malay *rindu* is better than 'yearning'; it really grips the liver.) *Asam kandis*, with all the acidity of its symbolism, sweet-sourish, literally brings the *tangis* (tears) to your eyes, as well as the juice of mortal life itself to your mouth. The second couplet merely states what has been foreshadowed - no, given the foretaste of - in the first: "The soul weeps at the edge of the grave" (literally on the edge, and on edge) "yearning to return to the earth".

Frank Swettenham wrote an essay arrogantly titled *The Real Malay*. This is how he describes his 'real Malay': "In his youth the Malay boy (sic) is often beautiful, a thing of wonderful eyes, eyelashes, and eyebrows, with a far-away expression of sadness and solemnity, as though he had left some better place for a compulsory exile on earth."

The Malay as a compulsory exile on earth? Or lives "as though" he was one? The *pantun* I just quoted clearly gives the lie to this piece of sentimental Orientalist fantasy. But then, there are Malays who apparently share this fantasy. The *pantun* is clearly a this-worldly *pantun* to me. But if you turn to *Kumpulan Pantun Melayu* (published by Dewan Bahasa), the most comprehensive *pantun* collection available, you'll find it placed in the section of *pantuns* on religious themes!

I can imagine the editor, deaf to the music of the earth that the *pantun* vibrates with, giving it a perversely pious reading. Something like this: the soul is crying at the edge of the grave because it's terrified by the visions of hell fire, and wants to return to the earth because it would like be given a second chance, not to enjoy life, but to do the *ibadat* (pious deeds) it had failed to do when alive! As if to confirm this reading another version of the *pantun*, a sort of bastard sibling of the first, is given in the same section. This one

155

could only have been invented by a *lebai* (pious elder). A beautiful earthy *pantun* was 'converted' into a sentimental lump of piety. Here it is: "*Asam kandis asam gelugur/ Ketiga asam si riang-riang/ Menangis mayat di pintu kubur/ Teringat badan tidak sembahyang.*" The second couplet ("The corpse weeps at the door of the grave/ Remembering the prayers it had failed to perform in life.") must have served well in *khutbahs* (sermons). But anyone with an ear for poetry could see that even here the imagination of the suppressed instinct slyly asserts itself. Poetry always triumphs over preaching: *si riang-riang* (cicada; what an earth-bound yet gloriously outspreading sound!) poetically 'mocks' its rhyming word in the last line. The opening couplet here, instead of foreshadowing in terms of sound the meaning of the second couplet, as is usual in the *pantun*, actually 'undermines' it. This is Malay ambiguity par excellence.

Anybody who claims that the Malay is a compulsory puritanical exile on earth must have a fantasy Malay in mind. My Malay loves this world with all the pleasures it has to offer. And if he is a natural poet, he can - or at least he used to - celebrate it in language that vibrates with sensuous openness, without any sense of shame or guilt. Some of the hedonistic and erotic *pantuns* are really quite remarkable. For a taste of them I'm afraid you'll have to wait till next week.

Salacious Pleasures of Pantuns

[29th May 1991]

LISTEN to this pantun:

> *Tanam padi di Bukit Jeram*
> *Tanam keduduk atas batu*
> *Macam mana hati tak geram*
> *Menengok tetek menolak baju*

And my translation:

> Plant the padi with a thrust
> Stroke the seedlings with dew
> It drives you crazy with lust
> To see the tits tilting the *baju* (blouse)

(Note: The first couplet is a very free rendering of the original.)

The puritan will no doubt dismiss this *pantun* as 'obscene' and therefore unworthy of being part of the treasured heritage of the race. Unfortunately for our friend, the 'offensive' pantun is included in *Kumpulan Pantun Melayu* (A Collection of Malay Pantuns), published by that august body, Dewan Bahasa dan Pustaka. I think this pantun is marvellous. Its very simplicity and directness, directness to the point of possible 'vulgarity', heightens its erotic appeal; paradoxically, there is a kind of subtlety in its stark salaciousness. What's more, its eroticism is, in my perhaps eccentric reading, not of the limiting kind. Properly read, with the mind alert to the semantic and cultural resonance of the key words, you'll see more than the surface evocation. In the *tetek menolak baju* (literally, tits pushing at the blouse), much more than a lovely pair of *tetek* (breasts) is revealed. I'd even say a whole world is seen to revolve on the tip of each *tetek*, on the point of each *puting* (nipple), or better still, *mata susu* (the eye of the breast). And a whole world view is suggested by *geram* (feel excited for, passionate for). The foreshadowing word *Jeram* (here the name of

157

a hill, but literally 'cataracts' or 'rapids') heightens the sense of life as rapids, and thus reminds us that one simply must seize the moment as it flies. *Geram! Carpe diem!* To see the *tetek menolak baju* in this pantun is almost like seeing a Blakean "World in a grain of sand,/ And a Heaven in a wild flower,/ Hold(ing) Infinity in the palm of your hand,/ And Eternity in an hour ..." Absurd 'Sallehcious' hyperbole? Perhaps.

The central word of the pantun, *hati* (literally liver, but the English equivalent here would be heart), is also the key word in Malay folk physiology. The liver to the Malays is traditionally the seat of the passions. (This was also the case in ancient English belief; you can find it surviving in Shakespeare's plays and poems.) The *hati*, the organ that conceals the secret of the Malay as a creature of feelings and passions, is vital to any attempt to understand the race. If you want to know what the *hati* is to the Malay, soak yourself in the pantuns. Only the *hati* can feel *geram* the way a Malay feels it, only the *hati* can generate it. None of the English equivalents for *geram* can match the fierce ambivalence of the Malay word. *Geram* is ambivalent because there can be an element of ferocity, even violence in the desire. The rhyming of *Jeram* and *geram* in the above pantun not only heightens the sense of *carpe diem* (Latin for 'seize the day'), but also strengthens the ambivalent ferocity of the desire. *Menolak* (pushing, rejecting), is also seductively ambiguous. You can see the *tetek* (what's breasts, busts, tits, even bosoms compared to the alliterative disyllabic *tetek?*) - you see the *tetek*, and the nipples pushing the *kebaya* (the *baju* simply has to be a *kebaya*), making the tight tighter, the stretched more stretched; and at the same time you have a flashing vision of the *kebaya* being violently stripped, pushed away, off the body - in other words, rejected. And the first couplet, the part of the pantun known as *pembayang* (foreshadowing), which in the best pantuns gives you through sound and imagery the foretaste of the meaning stated in the second couplet - well, this particular *pembayang*, this foreshadowing couplet truly, poetically and concretely enacts the foreplay of the anticipated coupling. What more can you want? That itself? Well ...

Talk of foreshadowing couplet enacting the foreplay of the coupling in the concluding couplet, listen to this:

Di mana kuang bertelur
Di atas lata di celah batu
Di mana abang nak tidur
Di atas dada di celah susu

Where does the dove lay its eggs
In the rapids between the rocks
Where may I lay my head, my love
On the chest between the breasts.

(Note: *kuang* is actually pheasant; I'm sorry to have to sacrifice it for reason of poetic necessity.)

There is a well-known saying: *ikut hati mati; ikut rasa binasa* (to give rein to one's passions means death; to give rein to one's feelings means destruction). Here too my manic mind can detect a hidden ambivalence. This saying is usually taken as a stern warning against listening to the dictates of the heart, of the liver. In a sense, and on the surface, yes; but if you listen to the hidden *hati* of the saying, to the surging of the ancient blood in the subterranean veins of its meaning, you'll hear ancestral voices prophesying spiritual and metaphorical bodily death to the race if it keeps on denying its instincts for life, freedom and joy. Hang Jebat knew that; he heard the ancestral voices in his *hati* and did what he felt he had to do. His *hati* simply refused to *mati* (die), even at the expense of the body. *Tepuk dada tanya selera* (slap your chest and ask what your appetite is like). That's what Jebat would say, taking the saying in his characteristic individual way.

In my reading, which I imagine Jebat would endorse, the saying doesn't necesssarily mean "look before you leap", as it is normally taken to mean. This common interpretation is, I believe, another instance of life-avoiding caution insidiously supplanting the original dare in the psyche of the race over the centuries of historical development. The insidiousness of this silent contagion of the spirit was such that the modern Malay can only hear the tone of caution in the saying. The other tone its opposite, which is 'hedonistic' (for this saying is actually ambiguous), is to me much stronger. I can imagine Jebat saying it with a ringing voice, his clenched fist beating against his burning breast. Note that *dada*, literally breast, can also be a synonym for *hati*, and *selera*, literally appetite, can also mean zest for life (*selera* in the *hikayat* is sometimes a poetical name for the body). But then even the most defiant line can be emasculated by the emasculated. The emasculated is someone whose *hati* has become atrophied. The puritan is an example of a person whose *hati* has become atrophied; for in order to become a true liver, meaning open to the marvellous possibilities of life, your *hati* (liver, remember) has to be alive. Always looking before you leap can be dangerous for the spirit. Jebat knew that. And never listening to your *hati* when it's *sakit* (sick), always ignoring the complaints of the liver, can be fatal for the liver. Jebat knew that too. *Sakit hati* (literally 'sickness of the liver') is always associated with the amok and the lover blighted in love. Remember that. And remember too that the amok is not always a mad zombie who runs amok without any rhyme or reason. Don't ignore your *hati* when it's *sakit*. Don't repress or betray the cries of your instincts, your body, your spirit. If you do that, you might run amok or, it there's nothing left in the liver to fuel an amok, you'll just die in life and become a liver without a living liver.

Only the living liver can feel the kind of passion expressed in this marvellous and powerful pantun:

> *Kerengga di dalam buluh*
> *Serahi berisi air mawar*
> *Datang hasrat di dalam tubuh*
> *Tuan seorang jadi penawar.*

> Red ants crawling in bamboo shaft
> Vessel brimming with rose water
> When my body's possessed by lust
> Only you can be the appeaser.

A race that can produce a pantun so passionately compact as this, coupling the crimson ferocity of sheer lust, embodied by the image of the red ants in the bamboo shaft, with the lovely tenderness of diaphanous desire, suggested by the fluid vowels, the assonance, as well as the imagery of *serahi berisi air mawar* (*serahi*, vessel, and *berisi*, filled) so sensuously, seductively flowing into the unspoken *berahi*, lust, desire - this race cannot be a stranger to sexual hedonism, however you define that word.

If it is true that hedonism was part of the essential nature of the race, what has happened to it? If in fact it is no longer a determining force in his being, is it still lurking in the subconscious, kept suppressed there by some bigger alien force? By way of suggesting possible answers, I'll give you a parting pantun:

> *Ke Teluk sudah, ke Siam sudah*
> *Ke Mekah saja aku yang belum*
> *Berpeluk sudah, bercium sudah*
> *Bernikah saja aka yang belum.*

> I've been to Thailand, to the Gulf too
> Only to Mecca I haven't been
> Kissed them I have, and known them too
> Without going through the wedding scene.

Luna, Lunacies and Lovers

[28th October 1992]

In *Body Time,* Gay Gaer Luce says: "Of the many rhythms we casually observe in the creatures around us, the most familiar is the daily rhythm of activity and rest."

I'd add to that: Among lovers, the time for rest can be a time for a specially passionate activity. Like sex at siesta time, for example; those who have done it tell me it can be quite fun. Properly approached, preferably with ritualised foreplay - that and some sense of the essential sacredness of the occasion can do wonders. So I'm told. Gay Gaer further says: "Dogs, diurnally active like man, will follow their owners to bed." What happens in the bedroom Gay Gaer doesn't say. She simply goes on to talk about cats whose rhythm is very much like man's: "lazy by day," cats "find the onset of darkness stimulating, and then begin to play." Cats' sense of foreplay is quite exciting for man to watch and get ideas from. If sex at siesta time can be fun, it can even be more so at the time of the lunar eclipse. I've never tried it, but I can imagine how it can be so, considering that the rhythm of a woman's body is so tied up with that of the moon. (The Malay word for menstruation is *datang bulan* (the moon comes), another instance of the tendency of Malay to be literal and metaphorical at the same time.)

If you don't believe me read *Kekasih* (Beloved), Usman Awang's marvellous, erotically charged love poem. Now I know why Usman Awang at one time had Tongkat Waran (police baton) as a pseudonym. It symbolises not only his passionate commitment to the cause of the poor and the betrayed (he himself comes from a very poor family), but his remarkable poetic virility and sensuality in his rare ventures into the difficult genre of love poetry. I said "rare ventures" because the lover in Usman the poet is not so prominent as popular notions about him would have it, and certainly not as conspicuous as the politically committed writer. In the whole of his collected poems, *Puisi-puisi Pilihan*, there is only one real love poem,

162

Kekasih. But this one poem is near-perfect. It was written in the early Seventies and is one of the best poems Usman has written. I consider it one of the very best love poems in the language, fit to be in the virile company of those erotic *pantuns* celebrated in this column some time ago (see *AIP*, May 13 and 29, 1991).

Compared to the mush and gush of the purely verbal sentimental *penyairs* (poets), who can pen a 'love poem' at the drop of a sarong, Usman's *Kekasih* stands out like the magnificent and inspiringly seductive tits of Gunung Ledang. And it is not surprising that when the Suasana Dance Company wanted a poet to celebrate the legend of Puteri Gunung Ledang, it turned to Usman Awang. The poem that Usman wrote is called *Kunang-kunang Gunung Ledang*, after the Ezanine Ahmad dance drama which was staged in Kuala Lumpur recently.

Before we look closely at *Kekasih*, here's the poem in its entirety:

> *Akan kupintal buih-buih*
> *menjadi tali*
> *mengikatmu*
>
> *akan kuanyam gelombang-gelombang*
> *menjadi hamparan*
> *ranjang tidurmu*
>
> *akan kutenun awan gemawan*
> *menjadi selendang*
> *menudungi rambutmu*
>
> *akan kujahit bayu gunung*
> *menjadi baju*
> *pakaian malammu*
>
> *akan kupetik bintang timur*
> *menjadi kerongsang*
> *menyinari dada mu*
>
> *akan kujolok bulan gerhana*
> *menjadi lampu*
> *menyuluhi rindu*

163

akan kurebahkan matari
menjadi laut malammu
menghirup sakar madumu

Kekasih, hitunglah mimpi
yang membunuh realiti
dengan syurga illusi

The right approach to this poem is by way of an earlier work, *Kelopak Rasa*. Or better still by way of *Kelopak Rasa* and those anonymous erotic *pantuns* like the ones I discussed in this column last year. Familiarity with the *pantuns*, in fact, is an absolute must for an appreciation of Usman's poetry; the continuity of sensibility and aesthetics between the tradition of the *pantun* and the modern Malay poetry is best revealed in his work. Dr Lloyd Fernando, in his introduction to one of Usman's volumes, rightly points out that *rasa* (feelings, sensitivity, sensibility) in his poetry has an almost metaphysical quality. In the words of *Kelopak Rasa* itself, it is an *anugerah keramat* (sacred gift); another word for it is *barakah* (poetic grace). Rasa in this sense informs and universalises Usman's passion both as a love poet and as a poet-spokesman of the insulted and the injured. *Rasa* is what makes *Kekasih* both delicately sensuous and powerfully charged with eroticism. The poet can effortlessly range from the cosmic to the concrete, in effect uniting the two in one experience. The entire universe, from the foams on the ocean waves to the stars and moon, participates in this fervent expression of love and desire. Right from the opening line, the cosmic embrace of the poet's desire is given concrete expression almost unbelievably erotic in its effect. "*Akan kupintal buih-buih/ menjadi tali/ mengikat mu*". Abidah Amin's translation of the opening verse ("I'll twine the froth of the sea/ into a rope/ to tie you") is quite good, but you need to be able to read the original to fully feel its erotic power. The same is true of the following verses. The verbal music of the original ("*Akan kutenun awan gemawan/ menjadi selendang/ menudungi rambutmu*") is very difficult to carry over into English. Malay has a kind of easy euphony that can be treacherous to the poet who lacks the artistic discipline as well as depth of feeling.

Here's Adibah's English version of these stanzas: "I'll spin the clouds/ into a veil/ for your bedchamber/ I'll sew the mountain winds/ into a nightgown for you/ I'll pluck the star of the East/ a brooch to sparkle/ on your breast/ I'll bring down the darkened moon/ a lamp to light/ my desire/ I'll sink the sun/ embrace your seas of night/ drink your crystals of honey." The images are fine, the syntax adequately reflective of the original. But I feel the translator's decision (if it was a conscious decision) to stay close to the original rather than exercise the freedom of 'transcreation' has resulted in her English version being rather weak in terms of rhythm and verbal music.

The truly marvellous verse six ("*Akan kujolok bulan gerhana/ menjadi lampu/ menyuluhi rindu*") is ... well, literally untranslatable: "bring down" doesn't have the concrete aggressive connotations of *jolok* (to poke in order to bring down). And the *sakar* (sugar or sweet stuff) in verse seven is a delightful near-pun (*zakar* means penis) which is totally lost in the English version. It is a testimony to the poet's deep intimacy with *rasa*, the *anugerah keramat* (sacred gift) he is blessed with, that with just one poem he leaves the sentimental verbalisers far behind, drowned in their easy-come-easy-go so-called 'love poems'.

Brother Henri, Honorary Malay

[17th July 1991]

Recently a 1930 classic, set in old Malaya and written by a Frenchman, was reprinted by Oxford University Press. It is called *Malaisie* (English translation: *The Soul of Malaya*), and the author is Henri Fauconnier. I used to think it's the best book ever written by a European about the Malays. I still think it is, but my feelings about it today are a bit more complicated than they were when I first read it almost thirty years ago.

Fauconnier was a rubber planter in Selangor early this century. His book, first published in 1930, is a semi-autobiographical novel. It paints an interesting, at times rather comical, picture of life on a plantation during that period; and the clubby British planters are treated with wry irony. It is a good book with some historical value, but to me its main interest lies in its insight into the Malay psyche and sensibility. The story has only a loose plot in the conventional novelistic sense, and this plot is really developed and acquires some elements of excitement only in the last third of the novel when the main Malay character runs amok. There is a lot of extended ruminations and conversations about the meaning of life, the nature of the Malays, the uniqueness of the Malay language, and the aesthetics of the *pantun* and so on. The story is really about the education of the narrator, a young untested planter named Lescalles, who acquires a deeper knowledge of life and of the Malays through his friendship with a mysterious recluse, Rolain, whose plantation he manages.

A reader familiar with Edward Said's brilliant assault on Orientalism, and who is wised up to the romantic 'imperial' perversions in Western imaginative writings about the East will no doubt find certain things quite repugnant in *The Soul of Malaya*. This is how the narrator describes his mistress, Palantiai, wife of his Tamil gardener: "She let herself be stroked like a docile filly, and looked up at me with great deep empty eyes ... A woman is no more than a delicacy, sweet or sour ... The choice of sweetmeat that Malaya offered me, on behalf of India, resembled one of those chocolates wrapped in variegated paper and filled with sugary liqueur." One can argue, of course, that this is the perception of a character whose head is stuffed with Orientalist clichés about the East, and is not necessarily endorsed by the author. Rolain, who often seems to speak on behalf of Fauconnier, appears to be cynical at his protege's expense. He says to the letter, "You? For them (Palaniai and her apparent pimp of a husband) you do not count. You are beyond caste." But Rolain goes on, "Palaniai brings you merely a propitiatory offering, and Karuppan (the husband) troubles himself no more than men of ancient days who gladly gave their wives to a god with a taste for mortal women."

Despite the touch of irony there, the analogy of the "god with a taste for mortal women" is revealing of what Said would call latent Orientalism in this book. And the Palaniai episode is by no means an isolated case of this. Yet I would hestitate to dismiss the book as hopelessly contaminated by 'Orientalism'. Fauconnier is clearly a child of European romanticism, and that inevitably colours his perception of his Malayan characters and their values. But that doesn't necessarily mean he distorts everything he sees - in the form of romantic idealisation or unconscious condescension. It should also be remembered that his apparent spokesman, Rolain, is a character with very fluid views about life and man. Lescalles finds Rolain hard to pin down; his remarks are often allusive, and sometimes paradoxical, even contradictory. One gets the impression that despite the French-style philosophical sophistication of his talk, there is an unconscious attempt to absorb into it something of what he perceives as the peculiar allusiveness of the Malay mode of communication. While he can be memorably articulate about the Malays, he stresses that he "know(s) very few of the secrets of the Orientals". And, more importantly, he keeps reminding Lescalles that every idea or perception is provisional. He tells his protege that "men have settled ideas only on subjects they have never thought about". I must admit I find some of the things Rolain and his protege say about the Malays quite acute and suggestive. The passages on the Malay language, the *pantun*, and the character of the 'true Malay' reveal a mind that is deeply sympathetic. Is there beneath all this attempt to articulate the perceived reality of the Malays, an urge to 'appropriate' its otherness? If there is, the act of appropriation is, I think, inseparable from the act of creative imagination itself, specifically of the romantic imagination. And if it is 'imperial', it is so in the sense that the act of imagination itself is or can be 'imperial'; the political ideology of Western imperialism is probably incidental or coincidental to it (unlike the case of imperial writers like Kipling). I would imagine when we Orientals write about the Occidentals, our imagination can be 'imperial' too.

In *The Soul of Malaya*, you'll meet some of the common stereotypes about the Malays - our infamous indolence, our acute sensitivity to insult to our honour, our unpredictable violence, and so on. But in this book these stereotypes don't come across as stereotypes to me. There is something about the quality of the writing, and the sensibility behind it, that accounts for this. The main Malay character in the book is Smail, Rolain's servant and *de facto* tutor in Malay literature and manners. The portrait of this gentle, sensitive youth who out of hurt pride runs amok towards the end of the novel is delicately etched. Smail is a natural poet and a living demonstration of Rolain's most memorable remark about the Malays: "They say these people are soft ... Yes, soft - as dynamite." The build-up to the amok of Smail is powerfully done. And what is particularly worth noting is Fauconnier's rare insight into the psychology of the amok itself. He describes it as a "*lucid* (my italics) frenzy that can utilise all the resources of guile". In essence, it is "a self-liberation through revolt; a soul too ... humiliated by its conscious enslavement, at last turns in upon itself and accumulates so much energy that only the faintest pretext is needed to release it".

That, to my mind, is the best thing ever said about the much misunderstood phenomenon of the amok. It took a Frenchman with a rare empathy with "the soul of Malaya" to say it. " ... *en souvenir de mon père bien aimé, qui était presque devenu un Malais ...* " (in memory of my father who all but became a Malay ...). Helene Fontaine Fauconnier, the author's daughter, wrote that on the flyleaf of the French edition of *Malaise* that she gave me when I met her in Paris two years ago. Well, Saudara (Brother) Fauconnier, 'latent Orientalist' or not, I welcome your spirit into the fraternity of the Malay race.

The Lessons of *Turtle Beach*

[17 September 1992]

The Australian film *Turtle Beach*, which angered our government so much that it nearly caused a diplomatic break between Malaysia and Australia, was released in March. It turned out to be a real turkey of a film; both in Australia and the United States, it failed to draw the crowd. When my daughter Anna saw it in the second or third week of its short run in Sydney, there was, in her words, "a grand crowd of four" in the cinema. I suppose if I hadn't asked her to see it for me, she would have heeded the unfavourable reviews and stayed away. The reviews must have been pretty bad. How can one otherwise explain the disaster at the box office? For the film had fierce advance publicity in the media, much of which was gratis, courtesy of our very obliging government. If there hadn't been that free publicity, there might not even have been the "grand crowd of four".

I think there is a lesson here for us, meaning our government. If a foreign film, or book for that matter, is set in Malaysia and contains scenes which might tarnish our marvellous image among the nations of the world, try not to make a fuss about it. Don't draw attention to the offending film or book; in other words, don't give it free publicity. For there is usually nothing like a scandal, including a diplomatic one, to help sell a film or book. In any case, protests are usually futile; nobody really heeds them. And if they sound overdefensive or self-righteous, as they usually tend to, it can, in fact, make matters worse. The offended party can seem to be protesting too much, which can be read as having something to hide.

There is another consideration which our government should try to bear in mind before allowing offended pride, national interest or whatever to take charge of its reaction to any perceived offence. It should remember that governments of Western democracies, including Australia, have a slightly different notion of free speech. In Australia, the UK or the US, it's accepted as part of the freedom of creativity for a film or a novel to create characters and depict scenes which put public figures in a very bad light, or suggest new highly damning interpretations of recent events of national importance. As long as the fictive mode of the work is understood and the writer or producer takes care to remain within the bounds of the law, this freedom is considered essential to a creative exposure of the truth of public life. The book and film *All The President's Men*, about the Watergate scandal, or the more recent Oliver Stone movie *JFK*, about the Kennedy assassination, are two well-known works which exercised to the fullest the constitutionally guaranteed freedom of creativity. The US government may not have liked what they showed of the corruption of the system, but there was nothing it could do about it.

In the case of *Turtle Beach*, our government's reactions seemed to suggest that it expected the Australian government to ban the film. It forgot that Australia is not Malaysia where films or TV dramas cannot even show a policeman let alone a Minister taking bribes. Canberra was so anxious about KL's reaction that it felt compelled to "dissociate" itself from *Turtle Beach*. This was necessary because one of the financiers of the film was the Film Finance Corporation, a government-based body. If this hadn't been the case, I wonder if Canberra would still have made the statement, to 'dissociate' itself from something with which it wasn't 'associated' in the first place. I haven't seen *Turtle Beach*, but I have read the novel. From what my daughter told me and from newspaper clippings about the film that she sent, *Turtle Beach*, as film adaptations of novels often are, is a crude sensationalisation of a respectable work of fiction.

The novel, written by Blanche d'Alpuget, wife of an Australian diplomat and a former journalist, who was once stationed here, was first published in 1981 by Penguin Books (Australia). It won four Australian awards for fiction and has been reprinted a number of times. It is quite an inoffensive book, I think, even by our government's standards. I assume it hasn't been banned in this country, for I bought my copy here a few years ago. I have some reservations about the picture of Malaysia and Malaysians projected by this novel. In particular, I thought that the treatment of Malay/non-Malay relations is rather shallow, at times even tendentious. And I wonder why the novel doesn't have a single positive Malay character. (Poor d'Alpuget, to have spent some time here and not come across a single decent Malay! Yes, Blanche dear, we do have people like Tunku Jamie, that "brown frog of a nobleman", that repulsive specimen of royal philistinism, who has to have lessons in his own mother tongue. Yes, but ...) These reservations about the novel, however, aren't strong enough to cloud my judgment of its literary merit. I think it's quite well written and has a serious theme which on the whole is treated with intelligence, wit and some imaginative tact.

Here's an example of its wit that I can't resist quoting: "The government man said, 'Nobody knows where these animals (i.e. the turtles) live, but they build their nests in only three places in the world - Costa Rica, Surinam, and Terengganu.' His tone indicated that this was a victory for the Malaysian government, against some other governments. Thailand perhaps."

Our man in Wisma Putra whose job it is to go through any suspicious book with a fine-toothed comb, must have been pleased with that bit about "a victory for the Malaysian government" which probably cancelled any doubts about the book as a whole. *Turtle Beach* is not really about the Vietnamese refugee crisis as the fuss about the film may have led Malaysians to believe. It tells the story of an Australian journalist, Judith Wilkes, who gets herself sent to Malaysia to cover the boat people at a time when her own private life is moving towards a crisis. There Judith finds herself caught in an ambivalent relationship with two people: Minou, the French-Vietnamese wife of the Australian High Commissioner to Malaysia; and Kanan, a Malaysian academic. Minou too has an interest in the boat people, but, unlike the journalist's, hers is deeply personal. A wily survivor who knows how to use her sexual assets to get what she wants, she is a sort of 'Suzie Wong' with a surprising capacity for devotion and self-sacrifice. She has been waiting for the arrival of her mother and child on one of the boats (the child is from a previous association before her escape from Vietmam). She is in the habit of keeping a vigil on turtle beach whenever a boat is expected. Her reckless obsession is a diplomatic embarrassment to her 'sugar-daddy' husband. The Minou story ends tragically when she throws herself into the sea on discovering that her family isn't on the boat. All this is witnessed by Judith; what a scoop for an ambitious journalist out to strike out on her own without the encumbrance of a hubby! Kanan, whose physical beauty strongly attracts Judith, is a somewhat inscrutable Hindu. She discovers that he has more *karma* than courage when it comes to moments of decision, and more tolerance of evil than she can tolerate. Her uncomsummated passion for him fizzles out like an unexpected monsoon shower in the hard light of his 'metaphysical' (and pragmatic) detachment from the tragedy of the boat people.

The Malaysian government was angered by the film adaptation of the novel mainly because of a scene in it that shows villagers killing the boat people on Pulau Bidong. Actually, there is no such scene in the novel, though we do get characters referring to such incidents, and none of the references suggests that only Malaysians are guilty of this lack of human compassion in such a situation. The massacre scene, in particular, roused the ire of d'Alpuget who condemned it as a gratuitous departure from her novel. I'd imagine she would have no more love for other instances of the scriptwriter's spicing-up of the story with sensational 'Oriental' elements. And I doubt that the film retains any of the instances of moral distancing or objectivity found in the novel - such as the subjecting of the protagonist to implied criticism in the climactic scene. Here, the moral ambiguity of Judith's profession, with its obsession with "scoops", is highlighted when the captain of the boat that brought in the refugees points out to her that there is basically no difference between their professions: "'You and me the same. We make money from peoples,' he said and laughed, grating his handcuffs in the direction of the refugees." Yes, corruption can come in many forms. And Blanche d'Alpuget is good and frank enough as a novelist to see this and embody the awareness in the work.

Barbarians Among Barbarians

[14 April 1993]

Imagine a proudly patriotic Malaysian adrift in London's West End. He is piously clad in white *baju* (loose Malay shirt) and pants and wears a black *songkok* (Malay cap). He blunders into a bookshop. There he is, a bit lost amidst all the bewildering excess of books, books, books. He begins to browse. The title of a book catches his eye: *Amongst Barbarians*. It stirs something vaguely unpleasant in his memory. The writer, he notes, is English. He glances at the blurb and learns that the book is a play based on a case of two English drug traffickers who were sentenced to death and subsequently hanged in Penang a few years ago.

Amongst Barbarians? Barbarians? Our patriotic browser is deeply proud of what our country has achieved since *Merdeka* (independence). And, inspired by our Prime Minister, he has become acutely alert to any signs of presumptuousness and arrogance in the attitude of Westerners towards us. Who are they to be so high and mighty and self-righteous about how our country is run? They should mind their own backyard and stop playing the moral watchdog of the world. *Amongst Barbarians?* The "barbarians" here, he hoarsely whispers to himself, must be us, of course. Didn't the Australian media call us "barbarians" when those two Aussie drug traffickers were hanged in Penang a few years ago? And the British Press - didn't it also call us "barbarians" when those Brits were hanged for the same offence? The very case that has been exploited by this play? And he recalls that Australian film *Turtle Beach*. Didn't it picture us as blood-thirsty "barbarians" who enjoyed slaughtering helpless Vietnamese refugees trying to land on our beach? And for something even more recent, he recalls the terrible things the Australian media hacks said about the heroic escapades of Raja Bahrin; that model father who kidnapped his beloved children from out of the jaws of infideldom in the form of his former Australian wife. With all this in the mind of our patriotic browser, he must feel perfectly justified in dismissing this play with such an insultingly provocative title as a piece of neo-imperial dung.

He casts another glance over the blurb. Something else now catches his selectively alert eye. This play, says the blurb, is a winner of "Britain's richest drama award" (The Mobil Playwriting Competition). He immediately puts two and two together and comes up with the brilliant conclusion that this play is a part of a Western capitalist conspiracy. A conspiracy against assertive developing nations such as our Malaysia which want their rightful share of the big capitalist cake. His patriotic fingers quickly turn over the pages. Sure enough, his patriotic eyes immediately spot dozens of insulting lines in the dialogue: "... sentenced by a bunch of savages", "we're amongst barbarians ... ", "these f-ing Pakis!"

Barbarians! *They* are the barbarians, he snorts. This insulting *tahi babi* (pigshit) of a play is the work of a Western barbarian! What barbaric arrogance to call us barbarians! He's so livid he can't help muttering all this aloud to himself. The other customers in the bookshop must think he's mad. I'd like to make a humble suggestion to our patriotic friend: Shouldn't you read the play first before you fume and make a bar ... bar ... (sorry) bloody fool of yourself? Barks our patriot back to me: Read the play? Why waste my time? I'm sure it's no different from all those biased and self-righteous newspaper reports. The fact that this one pretends to be art only makes it worse, more dangerous. Want to know what I really think? I think this book should be banned, not read! I say: It's a pity you chose to have such a bar ... bar ... (sorry) blatantly unfair attitude to the play. If only you would suspend your judgement and take the trouble to read it, you'd discover something interesting; in fact educational. That is assuming you know how to read a play, and have heard of a literary device called irony.

You'd discover that the play is not what you assume it is; that the "barbarians" of the title is actually ironic - ironic at the expense of ignorant and pathetically arrogant Whites, not us 'natives'. You might also discover that when it comes to the treatment of contemporary events or issues there is a huge difference between the serious writing of a responsible playwright or novelist and the scribbling of a media hack. A writer of serious

174

fictional works is usually free from the kind of pressures or motives that compel a journalist to sensationalise a news report or write a biased commentary. Neither is he subject to the box-office considerations that can make a film-maker trivialize or sensationalize the subject of his film. (Compare, for example, the novel *Turtle Beach* and the film based on it.) It is not uncommon for the mass media of any country to sensationalize or distort the social, cultural and political realities of another country. Do not think that our own media is an exception. It's different with serious literature - if it's any good as literature, that is. A good novel or play is written with a sense of moral and artistic integrity. It's this integrity that ensures objectivity in the writing, especially when it depicts something topical and controversial about another society, another culture.

This doesn't mean of course the novelist or playwright cannot be critical of another society. He has as much right to be critical, and as critical as he likes, of another country as he has his own. And the country that is depicted critically in his work must be civilised, i.e. unbarbaric, enough to recognise his right to do so. Some distortion of facts or surface reality can creep even into a work of high moral and artistic integrity. But such distortions are usually not intentional; if they are, it must be because of artistic considerations such as the urge to depict some deeper truth or other. Now, take this play that my imagined Malaysian has so rashly dismissed as an insult to our national honour. I think the writer, Michael Wall (yes, he is real and so is the play, which was published in 1989), has done something that should make our Malay writers think a bit; in particular about the business of writing on controversial topical issues involving a foreign country. Imagine a situation in which the writer and the subject here are reversed. Imagine Michael Wall a Malaysian *sasterawan* (writer) and the subject of the play is two Malaysian drug traffickers facing a death sentence in a British prison. I wonder how many of those *saterawans* who are defensively sensitive to and hypercritical of what Western writers say about us can be as objective as Wall is in *Amongst Barbarians*.

Wall's play is a detached study of human nature caught in a crisis; it makes no judgement about the allegedly 'barbaric' law that precipitated the crisis, or the country or society that

175

produced that law. The irony in the "barbarians" of the title is dramatically (i.e. objectively) enacted in terms of nicely controlled characterisation and pointedly witty play of dialogue and tones. Yes, there are characters in the play who ritualistically mouth lines about "bloody barbarians" and all that; and about ungrateful and treacherous natives ("We give 'em everything, their f---ing legal system 'en all, then they go and turn on us"). But these characters are critically placed by the playwright; their ignorant and pathetic arrogance ("They can't hang a f---ing Englishman!"), their moral and spiritual emptiness - all this is brutally exposed by the play. The younger of the condemned men (Bryan) keeps butting his head hysterically against the hard reality of the law they have broken. "There ought to be a f---ing law against such laws", he moans. His more honest mate (Ralph) tells him to shut up about the law. "If the law's an ass", he says to the poor boy, "you're the shit that comes out of it." What kind of a "shit" Bryan is and why he is such a "shit" we can gather from the kind of family that 'shat' him. The play is not only about two pathetically inadequate souls facing the rope; it is also about a family or families that lack the spiritual and moral resources needed to cope with the tragedy in the family. Bryan's working-class parents (to whom the unhappy trip to Penang is like a trip to another planet inhabited by "Pakis" - all brownies being "Pakis" to them) and his frustrated bitch of a sister bicker with each other in their Penang hotel room while in his cell Bryan moans and curses, curses and moans. It's some family, Bryan's is: the bitch daughter can say to her own father, "Shut up you f---ing crawler"! Meanwhile in another room, Ralph's playgirl mother, though more humanly attractive than Bryan's mother or sister, and not at all racially self-righteous or arrogant, could only deal with her estranged son's fate by sniffing cocaine all day long - that, and sex with siesta with the gorgeous-bottomed Malay bartender.

In the final scene of this 'tragic comedy', the two families are shown drinking themselves into a stupor in their hotel room, while in the prison Ralph and Bryan are being executed. The execution is enacted in two brief 'cutaway' scenes that have the effect of a horrible counterpoint against the seemingly endless barbaric orgy of drinking and bickering. *Amongst Barbarians* is in a sense about the potential 'barbarians' in all of us. And it is worth recalling that the word 'barbarian' is from the Greek *barbaros* meaning 'foreigner' (apparently because the talk of a foreigner sounded *bar bar* - i.e. 'Greek' - to the Greeks). We are all, as members of the *human race*, 'barbarians' to each other, aren't we? 'Barbarians' amongst 'barbarians' - that's what we all are indeed.

Thus Spake the Great Malay *Minda*

[2nd December 1992]

On November 14, *UTUSAN Malaysia,* the leading Malay daily carried a report of a talk given by the professor-poet and Sasterawan Negara Muhammed Haji Salleh. The report was headlined: *Kikis sikap rendahkan sastera negara* (Don't look down on the nation's literature).

According to the professor: "The perception that the nation's literature is not as impressive as the literatures of Britain, France and Japan is not accurate." He went on to claim that "Malay literature is as impressive (*sehebat*) as the literatures of other countries". (Note the change from "the nation's literature" to "Malay literature".) I wonder why the professor suddenly decided to join the chorus of mindless self-congratulation that has been making itself heard loud and clear this past year; at least since a minister, launching a book at Dewan Bahasa dan Pustaka, proudly declared that Malay literature had produced writers worthy of winning the Nobel prize - yes, the Nobel no less. Coming from a minister, whose speech was probably written by some goon whose head was full of *semangat kebangsaan* (spirit of nationalism) but little else, the declaration only amused me. But when similar statements come from someone like Muhammad Haji Salleh, who should know better, being familiar with the literatures of the world, it is quite worrying. Before I go any further on the matter, let me make a few things clear. This is to reduce the possibility of misunderstanding by *sasterawans* (writers) of my actual attitude to Malay literature.

For a long time the Malays were noted for a virtue whose effect on the character of the race was regrettable. That virtue is embodied in the phrase *rendah diri* which usually means 'self-abasing'; thus *merendahkan diri*, 'to abase or humble oneself'. Sometimes *rendah diri* is used interchangeably with *rendah hati* to mean 'modest', 'unassuming' or 'unpretentious'. I think *rendah diri* should be distinguished from *rendah hati*; the former

178

restricted to mean 'self-abasing'; the latter to mean 'unpretentious' or 'modest'. Unpretentiousness or lack of self-importance is a genuine virtue, but not self-abasement. There are a number of Malay sayings and *pantuns* recommending unpretentiousness or discouraging self-importance or bluster - for example: *Laksana buntal kembung, perut buncit dalamnya kosong* (like a puffy old box-fish, with a bloated belly and nothing inside). But the sayings and *pantuns* on the virtue of unpretentiousness are not as many as those that recommend self-abasement and modesty of behaviour or ambition. It is revealing that in the Hikayats, a character when talking to another, especially someone of a higher social class, always refers to himself as *hamba* (literally 'slave' or 'servant'). This self-suppressing feudal mentality of the ancient Malay was reinforced by the many sayings recommending the dubious virtue of self-abasement or modesty of behaviour and ambition - sayings such as *Baik membawa resmi ayam betina* (it's better to follow the disposition of the hen), or *seperti cebol gilakan bulan* (like the dwarf longing for the moon), or *pantuns* like *Tebok awan berkelok-berkelok/ Tepi dijahit dengan renda/ Kayu besar jangan dipeluk/ Kalau gagah melucut dada* (briefly, don't try to embrace a big tree if you don't want your chest to be abraded). Clearly there is a big difference between self-abasement and lack of self-importance, or between ambition that is cripplingly modest and ambition that is based on a realistic estimate of one's abililty and resources. When the president of Umno, in his speech to the party's recent General Assembly, told the Malays to "think big", he was not talking of mindless ambition like that of Mat Jenin (the famous character of Malay folklore). Thinking big is fine if one has one's feet firmly on the ground, not like Mat Jenin the dreamer whose feet were on a slippery coconut trunk. And thinking big with feet firmly on the ground is not quite the same thing as the talking big that our *sasterawans* and their political patrons tend to do.

I've always believed that being self-critical, both as an individual and as a nation, is a healthy thing, provided it's not carried to extremes. I believe that the ability to be self-critical is necessary to any worthy ambitions or ideals, but those ambitions and ideals must be grounded in an honest and unclouded perception of one's ability, resources and what one has achieved so far; all that, and a clear-eyed understanding of the social and cultural milieu and traditions informing it. Being intelligently critical of the achievements of one's country's literature is not the same thing as looking down (*menghina*) on that literature, or belittling it (*memperkecilkan*), or, in the words of Professor Muhammad Haji Salleh as reported by *Utusan Malaysia*, *merendah-rendahkan martabat hasil kaya sastera negara*. The word *menghina* (which can mean 'to insult' as well as 'to look down on'), is interesting in this context; its usage by our *sasterawans* when reacting to criticisms of Malay literature suggests a touchiness that amounts to a complex - a '*hina* complex'. The *sasterawan* as a type is a creature of contradictions - he can be full of self-importance and boastful of his achievements or those of his country's literature, and at the same time he can feel *hina* very, very easily.

My view of Malay literature (both modern and pre-modern) is that it has produced some interesting works, a few of them quite remarkable and which could be considered major in status. But by no stretch of the imagination could it be considered as impressive (in Prof Muhammad's word, *sehebat*) as the literatures of England, France or Japan. To anyone familiar with the literatures of the world (both east and west), the claim is so ridiculous that it is not worth rebutting by reciting chapter and verse. I realise that literary and aesthetic values cannot be divorced from their cultural context, and that notions of literary greatness are not totally universal. A particular literary work in any particular culture can be written or expressed in a form alien to another culture and therefore can only be fully appreciated by someone familiar with the literary tradition of that culture. This is particularly so if we are talking about literary traditions as linguistically and culturally wide apart as those of Europe and Asia.

If the someone who is familiar with the literary traditions of a particular culture is a foreign scholar, then he must be able to transcend the values of his own native literary traditions and look at the subject of his study on its own terms, which means those of the literary tradition to which it belongs. If he can do this he won't easily dismiss a work regarded as a classic by a particular culture as worthless as Sir Richard Winstedt did with

180

the Malay classical romance *Hikayat Hang Tuah* which he called "an uncritical farrago of legends" and not much else. But this observation about the relativity of literary values is really applicable to traditional or 'classical' literatures; that is, if we are talking about Malay literature, for example, it can only apply to its pre-colonial part. In terms of form, modern Malay literature is largely influenced by the West. The short story, poetry, the novel, modern drama - they are all Western in origin. From the post-war craze for fictional realism to the current pursuit by one or two novelists of *realisma majis* (magic realism) - it's all Western (including Latin America). This formal influence has been reinforced by the influence of Western tradition of literary criticism. There is not a single Western critical or theoretical idea that Malay critics haven't heard of and applied with relish to local works. Thus, given the universality of modern literary forms and the critical values they imply, we *can* talk of essentially 'universal standards' when judging the achievements of any particular literature (at least the post-colonial or modern part of it). I would still maintain this despite all the talk that has recently been heard about freeing our literary values and forms from the neo-colonial prison of 'Western-centricism'. That talk is mainly noise - full of unexamined assumptions, contradictions and fashionable fantasies.

Talking of fantasies, I'm reminded of the recently concluded 'fantasy event' called Kuala Lumpur World Poetry Reading (Nov 20-23). This poorly organised second-rate event (even the Malaysian papers criticised it) that was billed as a potential rival of well-known world poetry festivals such as those of Rotterdam and London, is another example of our *sasterawans'* tendency to talk big but know little.

Afterword

As a Malaysian who was steeped in Malay-Islamic culture before being exposed to "Western" ideas, I may be able to contribute a useful perspective on Salleh Ben Joned's writings.

Salleh's newspaper column *As I Please* (the main source of the selected writings in this book) has enraged some and delighted others. It would not be accurate to say that "some" refers to Malay-Muslims and "others" to Malaysians of other races and creeds.

True, several Malay-Muslim writers, academics and assorted individuals have lashed out at Salleh through the media and other channels. Incensed by his blithe disrespect for totems and taboos, they have pinned various labels on him, the mildest being *Mat Salleh* - the Malay nickname for an Englishman. But in private debate, many from the same community admit that they enjoy the idol-toppling and that Salleh is salutary for Malaysian society.

For "Western" readers, Salleh may be reminiscent of the child who exclaims, "The Emperor's not wearing any clothes !" In Malay folk-tale terms, Salleh is Si Luncai, the peasant boy who shocks the palace by comparing his father's bald head with the king's. Salleh appeals to that part of the Malay psyche which loves to laugh at the stupidity of Pak Pandir, the self-deception of Pak Kaduk and the greed of the pseudo-pious Lebai Malang. As the other communities of this land have similar traditions, Salleh's irreverent wit is very much in tune with the spirit that has kept Malaysians sane.

A growing number of Malaysians share Salleh's fear that pompous self-righteousness will smother this lively spirit. He sees his *Malaya* (the name of the peninsula before Malaysia was formed in 1963; the word, as Salleh has discovered to his joy, means "freedom" in Tagalog, a language related to Malay) being shackled and shaped into a humourless society. And he states what he sees with a child's devastating candour.

A child whose vision remians unblurred by schooling and

socialisation. He sees through fallacies wherever he meets them, in "Western" as well as "Eastern" thinking.

Though Salleh claims just "a little knowledge" of Islamic thought, he has read judiciously in the field and has used his "God-given mind" well. His style of analysis, though learnt in the "West", is surely common to honest thinkers the world over. In him, intellect and intuition merge. The result is an understanding that cuts through dogma to the essential idea of the Compassionate Creator.

Despite years of staying and studying in the West, Salleh is very much part of the rural Malacca earth that gave him life. His roots have always been with him; he never had to look for them. His Malay, in poetry as well as everyday speech, is Malaccan in its earthy exuberance.

Hence his protest against the prudish prettifying of the pantun, that most "sensuous" poetic vehicle of a vital and "hedonistic" people. And hence his horror at the transformation of his native tounge into a jargon-ridden monster bristling with bombastic words borrowed from English. His parody of the grandoise literary-academic style in *Transformasi of a Language* is one of the most brilliant items in this book.

This selection of Salleh's essays and articles comes seven years after he first burst upon the Malaysian literary scene with his volume of *poems sacred and profane*. Reading (or re-reading) the two collections side by side has been quite an experience.

The variety is tremendous, as is the energy, which explodes barriers between East and West, mind and feeling, the spirit and the flesh, the sacred and the profane. The overwhelming impression is of a free spirit that rebels against deadening conventions in a passionate celebration of life.

Adibah Amin
Kuala Lumpur
Malaysia
15 July 1994

Two new titles from PROF. **SHIRLEY GEOK-LIN LIM** :

MONSOON HISTORY (UK £6.99, USA $11.99)
Poems selected from Modern Secrets & No Man's Grove with the complete
Crossing the Peninsula (winner of the 1980 Commonwealth Poetry Prize).
"The poet in exile, but a counter-exile that permits an embracing of all
contradictions." World Literatures Today

WRITING S.E./ ASIA IN ENGLISH: Against The Grain (UK £12.99
USA $24.99)
The ten chapters demonstrate that South East/Asian Writing in English,
Against the Grain of local speech, national languages and national canons,
have much to tell us about place and region, and also about the nations
that their imaginations press upon from the outside of linguistic borders.

Three from **K.S.MANIAM** :

THE RETURN (UK £5.99)
This novel of magical realism has become a Malaysian modern classic.
Ravi attempts to come to terms with himself by sustaining the classical
Hindu virtues of spiritual proportion, harmony and grace, and avoiding
the decay of ethnic civilization through his pursuit of social mobility.
"THE RETURN bids fair to take a place among the top two or three of
any published Malaysian/Singaporean fiction in English"
Ooi Boo Eng, Univ. of Malaya

IN A FAR COUNTRY (UK £6.99)
This post-modernist novel is a potent cocktail of cultures, race and
religions.
"The book seeks to free itself from the literary ghetto by addressing
national issues and departing from realism to do so."
Dr. Paul Sharrad, Univ. of Wollongong, Australia

SENSUOUS HORIZONS, four stories & four plays (UK £6.99, USA
$11.99)
The eight works explores the complex and varied lives of husbands, sons,
wives, and lovers, all players in a game as old as time.

IN THE NAME OF LOVE by **Ramli Ibrahim** (UK £6.99)
"This is daring theatre taking risks and living dangerously, reviving a spirit
that at the time subverts and affirms the cultural concerns it displays,
questioning and challenging, but never losing sight of that essential
theatrical quality:entertainment. The plays mark a major contribution to
South East Asia theatre, and one which will delight audiences everywhere."
Prof. John McRae (Univ. of Nottingham)

WAYS OF EXILE by **Wong Phui Nam** (UK £5.99)
This collection traces the development of the poet from student days to
early maturity in lyrical litany, honouring the Malaysian soul as well as the
geographical and spiritual ground of his country.

"Wong's poetic scenario is eschatological in that it discovers powerful
destructive forces at work in the natural and social world." Anne Brewster,
Towards a Semiotic of Postcolonial Discourse

AS I PLEASE by **Salleh Ben Joned** (UK £6.99, USA $11.99)
"Anybody who wants to understand cultural politics today should read this
book. Anybody who wants to understand Malaysia today should read this
book. And anybody who wants an insight into the confrontations of East
and West, of Islam and the secular or Christian world, should read this
book!" Margaret Drabble

SKOOB PACIFICA ANTHOLOGY

NO.1. *S.E. ASIA WRITES BACK !* (UK £5.99)

No.2. *THE PEN IS MIGHTIER THAN THE SWORD* (UK £6.99, USA
$11.99)
The principle of Postmodern/Postcolonial writing is to deviate from the
tradition and to develop a new direction of thought...The understanding of
a writer involves anamnesis in the psychoanalytical context, the free
association of ideas and imagery of the unconscious in situations past to
discover the hidden meanings of his life.

"The Skoob Pacifica Series has provided a means for many writers to reach
international readership...The Pacific Rim should not be seen just for its
economic importance but also for the emergence of writings in English that
call for recognition in the literary world." British Council, Literature
Matters

SKOOB *Pacifica* SERIES

Skoob Pacifica Anthology

is a quarterly publication featuring
contemporary writings of the Pacific Rim

The first issue
SKOOB PACIFICA ANTHOLOGY No. 1
S.E. Asia Writes Back !

Subscription of Five issues:
UK GBP £20 post free
Elsewhere GBP £25 post free surface mail

Subscription enquiries to Skoob Books Publishing Ltd,
11A-17 Sicilian Avenue, off Southampton Row and
Bloomsbury Square, London WC1A 2 QH
Fax: 71-404 -4398
Cheques payable to Skoob Books Publishing Ltd.
I enclose a cheque for GBP £_____

Please debit my Access/Visa/Amex account
expiry date _____

Signature _____

Card No.

Name _____
Address _____
_____
_____

IN THE NAME OF LOVE
a play in three flushes
Ramli Ibrahim

This range of language and richness of character are the perfect representation of the racial, cultural and historical mix that is present-day Malaysia. Tension is never far below the surface in these plays. There is a range of binaries and dichotomies pulling against one another: present and past, traditional and contemporary, provincial and city, violence and tolerance, insider and outsider.

Prof. John McRae
Introduction to
In the Name of Love

Paperback
U.K. Price GBP 6.99

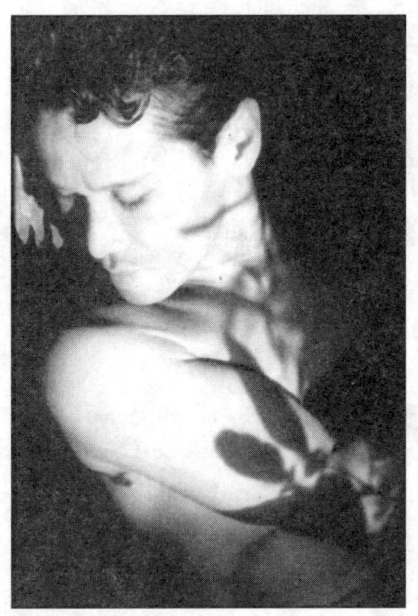

Skoob Books Publishing Ltd, 11A-17 Sicilian Avenue, off Southampton Row and Bloomsbury Square, London WC1A 2QH. Fax: 071 404 8398

Discover
MALAYSIA
With
Maybank
The Official Bank For
Visit Malaysia 1994
Maybank
VISA GOLD
VISA
Maybank
GOLD MasterCard
MAYBANK
Maybank
THE OFFICIAL BANK
Visit
Malaysia
Year '94

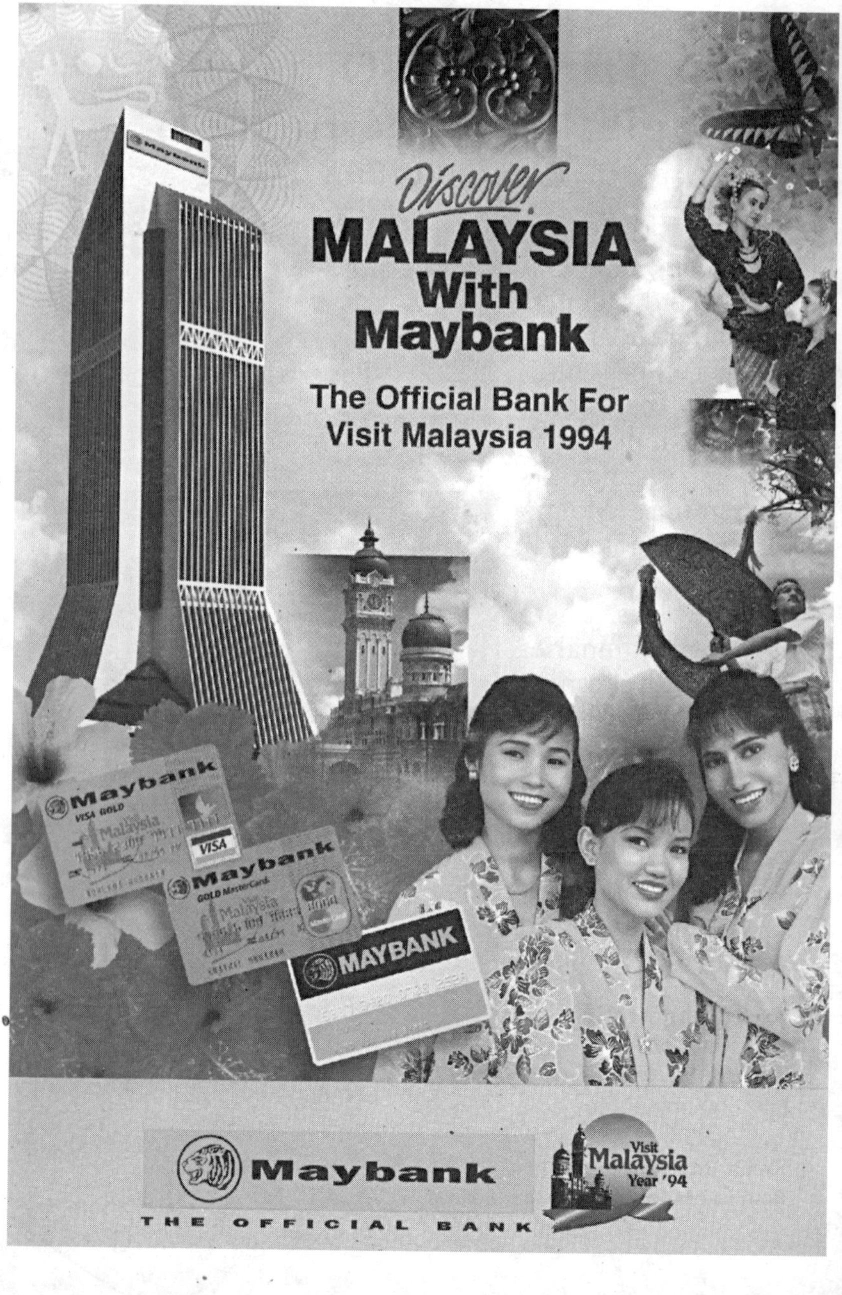

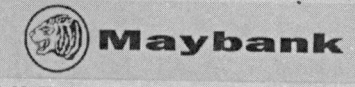

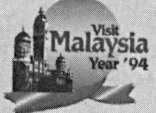